THREE BLONDES AND A BROWNIE

# Outrageously Delicious

## FAT-WISE™ COOKBOOK

*Nadja Piatka*

D0770285

Red Deer College Press

Personal Fat Budget Guide copyright © 1988 Minister of Supply and Services Canada. Used by permission.

Fat-Wise™ is a registered trademark of Three Blondes and a Brownie Inc. It indicates that the product has 50 percent or less fat than that of its regular counterpart.

To book speaking engagements, phone Listen International at 1-800-551-5476 or fax 1-403-423-4099.

*The Publishers*
Red Deer College Press
56 Avenue & 32 Street Box 5005
Red Deer Alberta Canada T4N 5H5

*Acknowledgments*
Edited for the Press by Patrica Roy.
Cover design by John Luckhurst/GDL.
Text design by Dennis Johnson.
Cover photograph by Don Hammond.
Text and author photographs by Brenda Bastelle.
Food styling by Allison Dreher.
Printed and bound in Canada by Webcom Limited for Red Deer College Press.

Financial support provided by the Alberta Foundation for the Arts, a beneficiary of the Lottery Fund of the Government of Alberta, and by the Canada Council, the Department of Canadian Heritage and Red Deer College.

*COMMITTED TO THE DEVELOPMENT OF CULTURE AND THE ARTS*

*Canadian Cataloguing in Publication Data*
Piatka, Nadja, 1949-
Outrageously delicious
ISBN 0-88995-158-6
1. Low-fat diet—Recipes. 1. Three Blondes and a Brownie
(Firm) 11. Title
RM237.7.P52   1996   641.5'638   c96-910310-7

*Ronald McDonald Children's Charities of Canada (RMCC) is an organization with a simple objective: to help children in need. It is committed to assisting organizations and individuals whose programmes are community oriented and focus on improving the quality of life for children and families of children with life-threatening or chronic illnesses and disabilities.*

*We all have a responsibility to help children in need and there is no greater joy than knowing that your efforts helped make a difference and improved the quality of life of a child. One of the reasons RMCC has been so successful in helping children and their families in Canadian communities is because of the cooperation and generous support we receive from concerned individuals and corporations.*

–RONALD MCDONALD CHILDREN'S CHARITIES OF CANADA

*Until one is committed, there is hesitancy, the chance to draw back, always ineffectiveness, concerning all acts of initiative (and creation). There is one elementary truth the ignorance of which kills countless ideas and splendid plans: that the moment one definitely commits oneself, then providence moves too. All sorts of things occur to help one that would never otherwise have occurred. A whole stream of events issues from the decision, raising in one's favor all manner of unforeseen incidents and meetings and material assistance which no man could have dreamed would have come his way. Whatever you can do or dream you can, begin it. Boldness has genius, power and magic in it. Begin it now.*

—GOETHE

*Dedicated to the memory of Arnie Nelson. A man of vision who had a joy and passion for life.*

*Author's Acknowledgments*

*Sincere thanks to the following people for making this book a reality:*

- *My teenage children Terry and Veronica, my proudest achievements*
- *My parents*
- *My sisters Lesia and Sandra*
- *Marie Peiffer-Mitchell for her constant encouragement*
- *Genoa Chadi Katz for her wisdom and fair sense of judgment*
- *Karen Jane Crawford for her friendship and support*
- *Beverly Feldman for setting an example of kindness and elegance*
- *Judy Schultz and the* Edmonton Journal *for giving me the opportunity to write my column*
- *Nick Lees, Wei Yew, and Yardley Jones for making my first book a reality*
- *Dennis Johnson for making this book a reality*
- *Nick and Kathy Kozak at Minit Car Wash for all the times you made me feel good about myself when I didn't*
- *Donna Karstad, Don Hammond, Allison Dreher, Brenda Bastelle*
- *And most importantly, to my partners and friends Terry Lynne Meyer and Candace Brinsmead, and their husbands Carl and Fraser. One never achieves their dreams alone. Thank you, Terry and Candace, for making mine possible.*

# The Three Blondes *of* Three Blondes and a Brownie:

## *Nadja Piatka*

**A**UTHOR of the best-selling book *The Joy of Losing Weight: The Nadja Piatka Method of Waist Management,* Nadja has long been an advocate of low-fat but tasty food. She is a certified fitness instructor, the creator of many hotel spas, and her nutrition column was a weekly feature in the *Edmonton Journal.*

Nadja, a single parent, began baking her muffins at home and testing them on her two teenage children. She was soon selling her muffins to local coffee shops, and when her customer base grew, she commissioned a local bakery to produce and deliver her products. Shortly afterward, Terry Lynne Meyer and Candace Brinsmead joined Nadja as partners, with Terry Lynne assuming responsibility for marketing and sales and Candace looking after finance and operations.

In July 1993, the three blondes invested $100 each to incorporate their baked goods company. Today, under their Fat-Wise™ trademark, their brownies and muffins are successfully sold through food distributors to restaurants, convenience stores, hospitals, and to charities as fund-raisers across Canada. They are the suppliers of Fat-Wise™ Muffins to McDonald's Restaurants of Canada.

Although their products are manufactured in three production facilities located in Edmonton and Toronto, they operate their business just as they did when they first started—out of their homes. They are an unconventional business threesome who choose to be close to their families whenever they can. "We once rented office space but never used it. Who's to say you can't make a successful business telephone call wearing a housecoat instead of a three-piece suit? The client never knows."

## *Candace A. Brinsmead*

**C**ANDACE spent seventeen years in the banking industry, the last few in senior management. Her many years in the industry, including international and commercial banking, have put her in great demand for the many financial seminars and television appearances to her credit. Candace is married with two children. Her interests include tennis, running, and eating, which bodes well for the low-fat desserts.

# Terry Lynne Meyer

**F**OR SEVEN YEARS, Terry Lynne was host of CFRN television's popular morning show *Day by Day*. In addition, she has hosted numerous prime-time, one-hour specials and variety programs. Prior to her broadcast career, Terry was an entrepreneur involved in the fashion, travel, and cosmetic industries, a certified fitness instructor, and an advertising executive. Terry was Miss Canada 1975, is married with three children, and feels that eating large amounts of Fat-Wise™ desserts is the best part of business.

# Contents

## Desserts

## Cakes, Pies, and Tarts

## Cookies and Bars

## Breads and Pastries

# Introduction

IN THE BEGINNING there was the two-Martini lunch. Steak and eggs were good for you, and exercise machines were vibrating belts that shook your fat off. Then it was discovered that we in the Western world were slowly killing ourselves. Obesity and high cholesterol levels were leading to all kinds of disease.

So to keep ourselves from an early grave, we mixed Perrier with our wine and jogged, swam, cycled, and walked. Entrepreneurs figured that anything the population did could be parlayed into fortunes, and exercise turned elitist. Smart clubs sprang up and were full of the Spandex-clothed climbing stairs to nowhere. If you hadn't run a marathon or had plans to do a triathlon, you were taking up space.

But, thank heavens, things have changed. We now know that to be fit we can eat delicious-tasting food and still lose weight. What we need is to get our hands on the right information. And that's the purpose of this book: to pass on to you the knowledge I have gathered by researching health spas, talking with great chefs whose dishes are dedicated to health and good food, and researching my column for a daily newspaper.

Doctors have discovered that when it comes to fighting disease, there's little difference between being moderately active and vigorously active. The secret is to make a commitment to active living; that is, work easy exercise into your daily routine. If you hoof it up a couple of flights of stairs, walk, or garden, you can reduce stress and cholesterol levels. You will also burn more calories than if you are sedentary, and as you know, to lose weight you must burn more calories than you consume.

Fat is a major foe because excess fat is stored in our bodies. Food guides indicate that no more than 30 percent of dietary intake should consist of fat, and with a little knowledge and planning, it's easy to reduce weight if you reduce your fat intake to about 20 percent. The Personal Fat Budget Guide in this book will help you calculate how many grams of fat you are allowed as well as provide you with information on the grams of fat found in the foods you eat. You may be surprised to discover how many hidden fats you consume. For example, if you think a muffin is a low-fat food, I have a surprise for you. The average, commercial muffin has some 25 grams of fat, about half your daily allowance if you are on a fat budget of 50 grams a day.

Six-time World Triathlon champion Dave Scott goes as far as to rinse the fat from his cottage cheese, but I suggest you never forget to enjoy what you are eating. To be extreme or cut back on meals leads to binge eating. We've all been there. On the way home from work, we know exactly what we are going to do as soon as we open the refrigerator door.

I believe in subscribing to the 80–20 formula: 80 percent of the time you must monitor your food intake; the other 20 percent enjoy what you want, when you want it. Getting to your desired weight doesn't mean denial.

Eat small portions regularly. To get the day off to a good start, eat a good breakfast. Research indicates that those who skip breakfast have a 5 percent lower resting metabolic rate (RMR) than those who don't. Sadly, surveys show that one in five Canadians (and just over half the American population) have nothing more than tea or coffee for breakfast. Enjoy a bowl of cereal and fruit for breakfast, and plan a healthy midmorning snack. The most filling snacks are often grain products such as low-fat muffins and breads.

For lunch, think grains, soups, salads, and fruit.

For supper, plan a medium-size meal using such ingredients as pasta, potatoes, rice, grains, and breads. Try to get meat down to a deck-of-cards size. Tuck into vegetables and fruits. Be careful of the decorations; they cause the trouble. Don't lather margarine, gravy, or sour cream on your food. Plan a nutritious late-night snack instead of devouring whatever is in the refrigerator.

If exercise is combined with more sensible eating habits, weight will be lost more quickly. Swimming and yoga are great for toning, but to burn fat you must get those big leg muscles moving. Running, cycling, and walking are ideal. It's also worth noting that covering the same distance running or walking will burn the same number of calories, but run or walk for the same amount of time and running will burn more calories. Don't forget that muscle loss is one of the major contributing factors to weight gain as you age. One of the best ways to maintain muscles is to begin a weight training program. And remember, muscles at rest still burn calories.

The rewards of a lifestyle change are enormous. Studies show that those who eat well and exercise regularly enjoy greater self-esteem, sleep better, and have more energy, and if that's not enough, they can always treat themselves to a pair of pants in a smaller size.

Traveling can involve changes in eating and exercise patterns that present problems to otherwise healthy eaters. The food usually served on airplanes, trains, and at highway rest stops is notorious for being high in fat. It's amazing how we will tolerate pancake-wrapped sausages while soaring at 35,000 feet. An alternative low-fat meal consisting of poached chicken and canned peas still swimming in water is enough to force conscientious travelers to pack their own snacks. Consider the following healthy items while in the airport or along your vacation driving route: bagels, rice cakes, fruit, vegetables, vanilla wafers, graham crackers, ginger snaps, licorice, popcorn, and pretzels are just a few of the treats you can enjoy while traveling.

Don't attempt to lose weight while on vacation. Just be content to hold your own by following these steps:

- If your holiday includes a meal plan, do not attempt to eat everything in order to get your money's worth. Order grilled fish. The seafood at most holiday spots is wonderful. Avoid disappointment and skip the dessert buffet. It always looks better than it tastes.
- Choose a hotel with health facilities and take advantage of them.
- Walk whenever possible. Take in the sights on foot (or bicycle) like the locals do.
- Do not bargain away future time with statements such as "I'll start a diet after I get home." Stay in tune with your body by considering your health needs, and you'll return home as fit as when you left.

Don't approach each special occasion or holiday season meal as if it's your last. If you eat a special occasion dinner at his folks' place, then your folks' place, then their folks' place, you'll end up eating a week's worth of calories in one day. Eat slowly and view each dinner as a snack rather than a meal.

Don't deprive yourself of your favorite holiday treats. Give yourself permission to savor small tastes of everything you like. If you lose control and blitz, forgive yourself so the despair won't fuel more bingeing.

What about those holiday drinks? Almost anyway you drink it, alcohol usually packs in 150 to 300 calories per serving. Beer and wine are at the low end while mixed drinks are higher. Switch to alcohol-free beer. It has about 65 calories per 12 fluid ounces compared to about 150 calories for regular beer and 100 calories for light beer. A 5-ounce glass of wine has approximately 100 calories and no grams of fat. Hard liquors range from 65 to 85 calories per ounce while liqueurs can have up to 110 calories and 4 grams of fat per ounce. Remember, the mix adds calories, too.

The winner for the highest fat- and calorie-laden drink of the season is eggnog. The classic version has 340 calories and 19 grams of fat per cup. This is not a problem if you do what I do. Buy the lighter brand of eggnog at the supermarket and mix equal amounts of eggnog and ice cubes in the blender. Process until the ice cubes are thoroughly crushed. Serve immediately. The thick, frosty drink will taste like a milkshake with only a quarter of the fat and calories of traditional eggnog.

Whether you want to lose weight or just start living a healthier lifestyle, the above tips combined with the following six easy steps to permanent, healthy weight loss will put you on the right track. After years of bingeing, starving, feeling deprived, and obsessing about eating, I finally learned that sensible, low-fat eating and regular activity is the only way to live. What a thrill it was to discover I could eat the most delicious food, lose weight, and never diet again! I lost 30 pounds forever. For me it was the same 30 pounds I had constantly battled. For others it may be 100 pounds and for some it may just be 10, but the frustration and obsession are the same. I want to share with you what I learned. Follow these steps and you'll soon see results.

### SIX STEPS TO PERMANENT, HEALTHY WEIGHT LOSS: A FORMULA FOR SUCCESS

1.  Cut down on fat. If you could make just one choice for improving your diet, it would be to reduce the amount of fat grams you eat. The *Canada Food Guide* suggests your diet should not have more than 30 percent of total calories from fat. Studies indicate that weight loss occurs when the dietary limit of fat is under 30 percent of total calories. Twenty percent is a realistic target to set for yourself.

    To determine how many grams of fat you should have each day, first determine how many calories a day you should eat. Choose your ideal weight and multiply by 15.

    Step 1:  120 x 15 = 1,800 calories.

    To estimate your personal daily fat budget, which will be 20 percent of the total calories, multiply 1,800 by 20 and divide by 9.

    Step 2: 1,800 x 20 = 360 ÷ 9 = 40 grams fat.

    I compare my personal daily fat budget to a piggy bank. It has only 40 grams of fat in it and that is all I have to spend. If I eat smart, I can be satisfied all day and never feel hungry. Or I can easily blow my fat budget on a handful of peanuts (50 grams of fat), still be hungry, and not lose weight. By learning where the hidden fats are, I can eat three meals a day plus snacks and still lose weight.

2.  Never overeat. This is called calorie overload. Whenever you take in

more food than your body needs in one load, it stores the excess energy in your fat cells. This also applies to calories from low-fat and non-fat foods. When a meal exceeds some 700 to 1,000 calories, the excess calories stimulate fat storage. The news gets worse. Studies show that calorie overload can actually create new fat cells. The more you eat, the more insulin is released into your system to reduce the level of excess glucose in your bloodstream. It converts the glucose into fat and stores it in your fat cells. Insulin opens up those cells and turns them into fat magnets. Not only are your cells taking in extra glucose, but all the fat you consume on your binge is also being pulled into those eagerly awaiting cells.

When insulin does a rush on your fat cells, they can't do what they normally do all day long—break down stored fat and release it into your bloodstream where it can be burned as fuel. Eating past the point of hunger isn't worth the price you pay. The last cookie you stuff in your mouth as you work your way down to the bottom of the bag never tastes as good as the first.

3. Increase your metabolism. If you've always wanted to know what your resting metabolic rate (RMR) is, here is your answer. This formula was created by Dr. Wayne Callaway, a well-known weight expert from the University of Washington. This example is based on a 46-year-old woman, 5'6" in height and 135 pounds.

STEP 1: Multiply your weight by 4.3 (135 x 4.3 = 580)

STEP 2: Multiply your height in inches by 4.7 (67 x 4.7 = 315)

STEP 3: Combine those numbers, then add 655 (580 + 315 + 655 = 1,550)

STEP 4: Multiply your age by 4.7 and then subtract that total from the sum in Step 3 (46 x 4.7 = 216 / 1,550 − 216 = 1,333)

That is the number of calories your body would burn if you did absolutely nothing but lie in bed all day. Your day should be a little more active than that, so you'll need more calories. To calculate how many calories you need in a typical day, simply add 30 percent to your RMR. If you exercise you may need to add 40 percent. Our sample woman would need 1,866 calories (1333 + 533 = 1,866).

The good news is that you can increase your metabolism in as little as three months by weight training. A 1994 study published in the *Journal of Clinical Nutrition* found that older adults who lifted weights three times a week for twelve weeks increased their RMR by 6 percent. Lead researcher Wayne Campell of Noll Physiological Research Center, Pennsylvania State University, found that because of the increase in RMR and the workouts themselves, subjects had to eat 15 percent more calories a day to maintain their weight. That meant an additional 100 calories a day.

When you weight train regularly you lose fat and gain muscle weight. I recommend not weighing yourself. The scale isn't as accurate an indicator of your fitness level as a pair of your favorite jeans. For each pound of muscle you gain, you burn an extra 75 calories a day to maintain it.

The need to maintain muscle mass starts in your midtwenties. That is when you start to lose about a pound of muscle a year. Since this natural loss of muscle lowers your RMR, you may gain weight as you get older. Studies overwhelmingly prove that you can offset this muscle loss and subsequent weight gain by regular weight training two to three times a week.

Aerobic exercise burns calories as you are doing it and plays an important part in weight control. Besides a workout program, include regular exercise into your day. Walk, dance, cycle, and climb stairs whenever you can. If you add just a few minutes of activity here and there throughout the day, you will burn fat. Studies show that just five to ten minutes of activity has a direct affect on your ability to handle stress, and when stress diminishes so does your body's tendency to store fat.

4. Don't undereat or skip meals. If you starve yourself, your body will respond by dramatically slowing down your metabolism. Anorexic women can burn 50 percent fewer calories a day than women who eat normally. It's the body's natural way of saving itself. Remember, too, that when you go on a low-calorie diet your body breaks down muscle needed to burn calories. Lack of food results in lack of energy, another side effect of dieting.

Skipping meals is another proven way of slowing down your metabolism. The minute you begin to eat, your metabolism cranks up to assist with digestion. By eating every three to five hours, you keep your metabolism elevated. Eating more frequently also prevents you from becoming famished, which usually leads to bingeing. You are more likely to choose junk food over something healthy when you are very hungry.

The last meal you want to skip is breakfast, truly the most important meal of the day. Studies show that if you skip breakfast (or lunch), you will probably compensate by eating a bigger dinner and indulging in more fattening late-night snacks. Since your metabolism is at its slowest at night, you are setting yourself up to gain weight. In fact, this is the pattern of most overweight people. They may not necessarily eat more, but they eat when they shouldn't. The greatest nutritional disservice you can do is skip breakfast. That is the meal that actually charges up your calorie-burning engine for the day. Dr. James Kenney of the Pritikin Longevity Center observes that "the vast majority of overweight people are far more likely to skip breakfast than thinner people."

5. Drink more water and less alcohol. If alcohol contains no fat, why is it fattening? A study conducted at the Institute of Physiology, University of Lausanne, showed that alcohol prevents the body from burning fat and actually increases fat storage. Alcohol raises blood sugar and insulin levels and stimulates the conversion of carbohydrates to fat. The Swiss researchers found that calories from alcohol are not similar to calories from carbohydrates, even though all alcohol is derived from grains, sugars, and fruit. The bad news about alcohol is that while it's being burned for energy, it prevents the body from performing its normal function of burning fat. The body's business of breaking down calories from fat is redirected to break down the calories from alcohol. Every ounce of alcohol consumed has the equivalent effect of about one-half ounce of dietary fat. Downing a couple of beers or glasses of wine every day for a month is the same as drinking a couple of cups of oil.

Alcohol can also stimulate your appetite. The average person consumes about 350 extra calories per meal when drinking. Where do all those spirit-related calories go? According to researchers at the University of California School of Medicine, right to your stomach and waist. They found that men and women who were frequent drinkers had larger waist-to-hip measurement ratios than those who didn't drink.

If you want to lose or maintain your weight and still drink, be sure to decrease your dietary fat intake to compensate for the alcohol. I compare drinking alcohol to eating dessert. I have dessert once in a while on special occasions, but I never eat the whole thing.

What you can't drink enough of is water. Your body loses about 10 cups of water a day. Since you get only 4 from food and metabolism, you need to drink at least 6 a day just to stay on an even keel. If you can drink the recommended 8, all the better.

Increased water intake can actually help get rid of fat deposits. Your body needs liquid to transport fatty acids into the bloodstream for delivery to your muscles for burning. The colder the water, the better. A gallon of ice water uses over 200 calories of energy to warm it to core body temperature. Whatever its temperature, always travel with bottled water in your car and keep a full bottle at your desk, so a drink is always just a reach away.

6. Create amazing results by making some simple eating improvements:
   - Subscribe to one low-fat cooking magazine.
   - Switch from whole milk (or 2%) to skim milk. Do it gradually by mixing them together at first.
   - Switch from cream in your coffee to milk, and you'll save 10 grams of fat per cup.
   - Sauté vegetables in defatted chicken broth instead of oil.
   - Order broth soups instead of cream-based soups.
   - Make your own cream soups by using nonfat sour cream or low-fat yogurt. For a rich soup base, mix nonfat dry milk with chicken stock or beef broth.
   - Remove the skin from chicken or turkey. The skin can be removed before or after cooking without affecting the fat content.
   - Use low-fat cheese instead of the high-fat variety.
   - Top your pasta with tomato sauce. Cream sauce pasta dishes such as Fettuccine Alfredo can have up to 60 grams of fat.
   - Avoid nuts. A handful of peanuts has as much fat as a serving of steak.
   - If you crave dessert, split it with a friend or eat only half.
   - Avoid crackers unless they contain 2 grams or less of fat per serving.
   - French fries cooked in healthier oil are still a poor food choice. Bake your own fries in the oven.
   - Salt your bread instead of buttering it. What most people miss is the taste of salt. A light sprinkling of salt may not be the perfect solution, but it does eliminate all the saturated fat.
   - Spread your sandwiches with mustard instead of mayonnaise. If it has to be mayo, make sure it's the fat-reduced kind.
   - Make your sandwiches with bread, preferably whole-grain, instead of croissants, which are 50 percent fat.
   - Use low-fat dressings on your salads. Some dressings add a whopping 30 grams of fat per serving.

- Don't consume unlimited amounts of fruit. Fruit is healthy but does have calories and a lot of natural sugar.
- Choose low-fat muffins and English muffins instead of regular muffins and Danishes, which have about 20 grams of fat.
- Use 2 egg whites instead of 1 whole egg in baking and save 6 grams of fat per egg. For an omelet, use 1 whole egg and 2 egg whites.
- Salsa is a great low-fat condiment; antipasto is loaded with oil.
- Have pretzels and air-popped popcorn instead of chips and nuts.
- Gingersnap cookies and Newton-type fig cookies have always been low in fat.
- Choose angel food cake instead of regular cake for dessert.
- The new low-fat frozen yogurt products just keep getting better. Have you tried some lately instead of regular ice cream?
- Satisfy your sweet cravings and snack on licorice. Red or black, a licorice stick has less than 40 calories and under a gram of fat.
- Drinking large quantities of sweet beverages can contribute to obesity. Even too many diet drinks can increase your appetite and insulin production, which in turn will reduce fat burning. Carbonated water with lime, lemon, or berry flavorings creates a refreshing, natural soda without any sweeteners.
- Start each meal with some low-fat protein such as skim milk, cottage cheese, tomato or lentil soup, or chicken. Then balance the menu with vegetables and complex carbohydrates such as pasta, rice, or bread. Many researchers regard the combination of protein and complex carbohydrates as heat-generating foods, which translates into burning more calories.
- Don't overeat. Overconsumption of any food—carbohydrate, protein, or fat—causes weight gain. And the very best way to add pounds? Overindulge before going to bed. You'll be sure to see results in no time at all.
- Get off the no-fat train to weight gain. Most low-fat diets produce an insulin imbalance that encourages fat storage in your arteries. This is caused by an overconsumption of carbohydrates and an underconsumption of good, monounsaturated and polyunsaturated fats.
- The final word in waist management is exercise. It's the secret formula, the magic pill, everything you've been looking for. It works!

I have collected my most outrageously delicious recipes for this book. Creating and testing them was truly a labor of love. I have also included the latest wellness information from the best weight and fitness experts in the world. Knowledge is a wonderful thing! Use what you will learn from this book to free yourself from agonizing over your weight, and start enjoying the benefits of a lean, healthy body.

# Appetizers

## Modern Dips

Where were you in 1954? That's the year Lipton came out with the king of all dips: the famous onion and sour cream dip. Combine one envelope of Lipton dried onion soup and mix with 16 ounces of sour cream. Add a bag of potato chips and there is your fat gram quota for the next day and a half.

Thank goodness the good old days of fattening dips are behind us. As a matter of fact, the same recipe with the same great taste can still be enjoyed just by substituting regular sour cream with nonfat sour cream. Simply blend with one envelope dried onion soup mix and enjoy with raw vegetables, low-fat chips, or baked tortilla chips. You'll save enough calories and fat to fit back into your old jeans.

# Hummus

*I've eliminated all the oil in this popular Middle Eastern dip, but you won't miss it. The flavor is enhanced by roasting garlic cloves and adding a touch of soy sauce.*

| | | |
|---|---|---|
| 1 | 19 oz (540 mL) can chickpeas, drained and rinsed | 1 |
| 1 | head garlic | 1 |
| 3 tbsp | fresh parsley, chopped | 45 mL |
| 2 ½ tbsp | fresh lemon juice | 35 mL |
| 1 tbsp | tahini sesame paste | 15 mL |
| 1 tbsp | low-sodium soy sauce | 15 mL |
| | salt to taste | |
| ¼ tsp | paprika for garnish | 1 mL |
| | sprig parsley for garnish | |

◼ Preheat the oven to 400 F (200 C).

◼ Remove the loose, papery skin from the garlic head without separating the cloves. Slice off ¼ inch (.5 cm) from the top of the head and discard. Wrap the garlic head in aluminum foil and roast for approximately 45 minutes, or until the garlic is very soft. Unwrap and cool enough to separate the cloves and peel.

◼ Combine all ingredients, except paprika, in a food processor. Add 1 to 2 tbsp (15 to 25 mL) water and blend until smooth.

◼ Transfer to a serving bowl and sprinkle with paprika. Garnish with a sprig of fresh parsley and serve with pita bread cut in wedges or fresh, raw vegetables.

MAKES 1 ⅔ CUPS

---

PER SERVING (1 tbsp/15 mL)
25 calories
1 g fat
36% calories from fat

---

# Roasted Eggplant Dip

| | | |
|---|---|---|
| ½ lb | eggplant (1 medium) | 250 g |
| 1 tsp | cumin seed | 5 mL |
| | pinch salt and cayenne | |
| 1 tbsp | fresh lemon juice | 15 mL |
| ½ tsp | fresh thyme | 2 mL |
| | – OR – | |
| ¼ tsp | dried thyme | 1 mL |
| ½ cup | fresh tomato, chopped | 125 mL |
| ¼ cup | fresh cilantro, coarsely chopped | 50 mL |
| ½ cup | plain low-fat yogurt (optional) | 125 mL |

Preheat oven to 350 F (180 C).

Cut whole eggplant in half. Place in a shallow baking dish, cut-side down, and roast for ½ hour, or until tender when pierced with the point of a knife. Remove eggplant from oven and allow to cool for 10 minutes. Remove and discard skin and stem of eggplant.

Mash eggplant pulp with a fork or process in a food processor. Combine pulp with cumin, salt, cayenne, lemon juice, thyme, tomato, and cilantro. Allow mixture to cool completely, then fold in yogurt. Serve with pita wedges, raw vegetables, or low-fat crackers.

SERVES 10

PER SERVING
*16 calories*
*trace of fat*

## Snacking

We used to believe that eating between meals promoted weight gain; now we think nibbling may help curb your appetite. When you eat lightly but frequently, a small amount of glucose courses through your system throughout the day. As a result, you won't get as hungry and may actually consume fewer calories.

Snacking may even be good for you, lowering cholesterol and reducing the risk of heart disease. In a study led by Dr. D. Jenkins of the University of Toronto, participants consumed 2,500 calories per day. For two weeks they ate three meals daily; then for two weeks, they ate the same kinds of food in the same amounts but spread out over seventeen snacks per day. On average, the snacking regimen lowered their total serum cholesterol by 8.5 percent and their bad LDL cholesterol by 13.5 percent.

Three meals a day is a social convention, not a physiological necessity. The body needs a certain number of calories and other essential nutrients daily and can absorb them in many small meals or several larger ones. If you prefer small, nutritionally balanced snacks during the day, there is no harm in such a plan. Just remember to eat the majority of your snacks during the day. Don't save them up for the end of the day when you are more likely to be inactive.

# Tuna-Artichoke Spread

*Did you know that a 6 oz (184 g) can of tuna has about 33 grams of fat compared to only 1 gram in the water-packed variety? Isn't it great being part of the nutritionally informed? You can share this information at those awkward moments when you've run out of conversation and are serving this savory recipe.*

*This is an easy and delicious way to add variety to your hors d'oeuvres platter. Serve with rounds of French bread or nonfat bagel chips.*

NOTE: *To prepare your own bagel chips, cut bagel in half, then cut each half into thin slices. Place slices on baking sheet and bake at 350 F (180 C) for approximately 5 minutes, or until crisp.*

| | | |
|---|---|---|
| 1 | 6 oz (184 g) can solid white tuna, in water, drained | 1 |
| 1 cup | artichoke hearts, in water, drained and chopped | 250 mL |
| ½ cup | low-fat cream cheese | 125 mL |
| 2 tsp | fresh lemon juice | 10 mL |
| 3 tbsp | capers, chopped | 45 mL |
| 3 tbsp | fresh parsley, chopped | 45 mL |
| ½ tsp | thyme | 2 mL |
| ⅛ tsp | cayenne pepper | .5 mL |

■ Combine all ingredients in a food processor and process until uniformly coarse. Refrigerate until ready to use.

MAKES 1 ½ CUPS

---

PER SERVING (1 tbsp/15 mL)
*35 calories*
*2 g fat*
*50% calories from fat*

---

# Spinach Cheese Strudel

*This recipe presents a new way to prepare phyllo pastry. The result is a crisper and less oily crust that won't become soggy when filled. Spinach has only 41 calories per cup (250 mL) of cooked leaves and is high in dietary fiber, vitamin A, potassium, and iron. This strudel appetizer is truly a crowd pleaser. I know because it is one of my most requested recipes.*

### FILLING

| | | |
|---|---|---|
| 1 lb | fresh spinach | 500 g |
| | – OR – | |
| 1 | 10 oz (275 g) package frozen spinach | 1 |
| ¼ cup | feta cheese, crumbled | 50 mL |
| ¼ cup | dry-curd cottage cheese | 50 mL |
| 2 tbsp | light Parmesan cheese, grated | 25 mL |
| ½ cup | green onions, chopped | 125 mL |
| 2 tbsp | fresh dill, chopped | 25 mL |
| | – OR – | |
| 1 tsp | dried dill | 5 mL |
| ½ tsp | garlic powder | 2 mL |
| 1 tbsp | fresh lemon juice | 15 mL |
| | salt and freshly ground pepper to taste | |
| 2 | large egg whites | 2 |

### PHYLLO PASTRY

| | | |
|---|---|---|
| 8 | sheets phyllo pastry | 8 |
| 1 | large egg white | 1 |
| 2 tbsp | olive oil | 25 mL |
| ⅛ tsp | salt | .5 mL |
| 2 tbsp | fine breadcrumbs | 25 mL |

■ Set oven rack on the upper level and preheat oven to 350 F (180 C). Lightly coat a baking sheet with non-stick cooking spray.

■ To prepare filling, wash fresh spinach and place in a large pot with water still clinging to the leaves. Cover and cook over medium heat until the spinach is wilted, about 3 minutes. Cool. Squeeze the spinach dry and chop. If using frozen spinach, thaw, drain, and chop.

■ Stir in cheeses. Add green onions to the spinach mixture. Stir in dill, garlic, and lemon juice. Season with salt and pepper. Beat egg whites lightly with a fork and stir into the spinach mixture.

■ Prepare phyllo pastry. In a small bowl, lightly beat the egg white, oil, and salt. Lay a sheet of phyllo on the work surface and, using a pastry brush, lightly coat the surface of the phyllo pastry with the egg white mixture. Sprinkle with ½ tsp (2 mL) breadcrumbs. Repeat this step, layering more sheets of phyllo on top.

■ Spread the spinach mixture along one end of the dough. Lift edges of dough near spinach and roll over to form a roll. Brush with remaining egg white mixture. Bake 25 to 30 minutes. Pastry should be golden brown. Remove from oven and cool slightly. Slice and serve.

SERVES 12

PER SERVING
*120 calories*
*4 g fat*
*30% calories from fat*

# Salad Rolls with Curried Peanut Sauce

*Invite some friends over to share these salad rolls. They can be served proudly as either an hors d'oeuvre or appetizer. This recipe was given to me by gourmet cook Maureen Hemingway, famous for her perfect dinner parties.*

| | | |
|---|---|---|
| 10 | 8-inch (20 cm) round rice-paper wrappers | 10 |

### CURRIED PEANUT SAUCE

| | | |
|---|---|---|
| 1 tsp | vegetable oil | 5 mL |
| 1 | medium onion, chopped | 1 |
| 2 | large garlic cloves, minced | 2 |
| ¼ tsp | cayenne pepper | 1 mL |
| 1 tbsp | curry paste | 15 mL |
| 1 tsp | tomato paste | 5 mL |
| ½ cup | fresh orange juice | 125 mL |
| ¼ cup | unsalted, dry-roasted peanuts | 50 mL |
| ½ tsp | fresh lemon juice | 2 5 mL |
| | salt | |

### FILLING

| | | |
|---|---|---|
| 10 | large lettuce leaves | 10 |
| 1 | large tart apple, peeled, cored and julienned | 1 |
| 2 cups | carrots, shredded | 500 mL |
| 10 | cilantro sprigs | 10 |
| 10 | green onions | 10 |

▨ Prepare sauce in a small saucepan. Heat the oil over moderate heat. Add the onion and garlic and stir well. Reduce heat to low, cover and cook, stirring twice, until golden, about 7 minutes. Uncover and stir in the cayenne pepper and curry paste until fragrant, about 1 minute. Add the tomato paste and cook for about 30 seconds. Pour in the orange juice and cook until reduced slightly, about 1 minute. Remove from heat.

### Body Image

*Brace yourselves girls! The Twiggy look has returned. Pick up almost any magazine and you'll see that thin is in. We wiser women of the 1990s won't buy into it this time, or will we? Surveys reveal that most women view themselves as overweight. In one survey, only 7 percent said they were satisfied with their bodies. What do most women want? Flatter stomachs, thinner thighs, no cellulite, slimmer hips, and better proportions. Maybe what we need is a reality check. We also need to encourage women to develop a positive self-image based on ability and personality rather than just physical appearance.*

*Before you decide to lose weight, take a good, hard, objective look at yourself. You may not need to lose weight at all but simply firm up some areas and get your muscle-to-fat ratio back in balance. If you do need to reduce body fat, maximize your health by making a few simple lifestyle changes. Maintain (or even build) lean body mass through regular exercise, and reduce the amount of fat in your diet. If the mainstay of your diet is fast food and dessert, that will have to change. You can still eat them but not as often. Stay healthy and learn to love the way you look.*

Place the peanuts in a food processor and chop very finely, almost to a paste. Add the curry mixture and process until a rich puree forms. Scrape the dressing into a small bowl and season with lemon juice and salt. Set aside.

To prepare rolls, soak rice-paper wrappers individually in hot water for 30 seconds to soften. If parts of the wrappers still feel firm, lightly moisten with a pastry brush.

To assemble the wraps, layer each rice-paper wrap with a lettuce leaf and spread 1 tsp (5 mL) peanut sauce over the leaf. Cover with apple, carrots, and sprig of cilantro. Lay a green onion over all and roll. Prepare remaining wraps.

These salad rolls will last at least four days, tightly wrapped and refrigerated. Serve with a low-fat, bottled plum sauce or sweet and sour sauce.

SERVES 10

PER SERVING
*56 calories*
*2.5 g fat*
*40% calories from fat*

# Italian Bruschetta

*Bruschetta makes an excellent hors d'oeuvre, appetizer, or snack. I often prepare it as a main course for myself when I am short of time and cooking for one. I included this recipe in my first book, but it's so popular I am offering it again.*

| | | |
|---|---|---|
| 1 tbsp | olive oil | 15 mL |
| 2 tbsp | onion, finely chopped | 25 mL |
| 1 | clove garlic, crushed | 1 |
| 4 | plum tomatoes, diced | 4 |
| | oregano, basil, freshly ground pepper to taste | |
| 1 tbsp | balsamic vinegar | 15 mL |
| 2 | cloves garlic, halved | 2 |
| 12 | slices French breadstick, ½-inch (1 cm) thick slices | 12 |
| 2 tsp | Parmesan cheese, grated | 10 mL |

▉ Heat oil in pan and sauté onions and crushed garlic until tender. Add tomatoes and seasonings to taste. Stir and heat thoroughly. Remove from heat and add balsamic vinegar.

▉ Under broiler, toast bread on both sides. Rub one side of hot toast with cut garlic. Spoon tomato mixture over hot toast. Sprinkle with cheese and broil for 30 seconds.

SERVES 4

PER SERVING
*190 calories*
*4.4 g fat*
*20% calories from fat*

# Mexican Green Chili Casserole

*If you are looking to serve a different type of appetizer, try this casserole.*

| | | |
|---|---|---|
| 1 cup | evaporated skim milk | 250 mL |
| 4 | egg whites | 4 |
| ⅓ cup | all-purpose flour | 75 mL |
| 3 | 4 oz (114 mL) cans whole green chilis | 3 |
| 1 cup | low-fat Monterey Jack cheese, grated | 250 mL |
| | – OR – | |
| 1 cup | skim mozzarella cheese, grated | 250 mL |
| 1 cup | low-fat old Cheddar cheese, grated | 250 mL |
| 1 | 8 oz (250 mL) can tomato sauce | 1 |

Preheat oven to 350 F (180 C). Coat a deep, medium-size casserole dish with nonstick cooking spray.

Beat milk, egg whites, and flour together until well blended. Split open chilis and rinse to remove seeds. Drain on a paper towel.

Mix cheeses together and reserve ½ cup (125 mL) for topping.

NOTE: *Do not rub your eyes or touch your lips while handling hot peppers. Wash your hands thoroughly afterward.*

Alternate layers of chilis, cheese, and cream mixture in casserole dish. Pour tomato sauce over casserole and sprinkle with remaining cheese. Bake 1 hour, or until a tester inserted into the center comes out clean.

SERVES 6

PER SERVING
*218 calories*
*6.1 g fat*
*25% calories from fat*

# Salmon Pinwheel Hors d'oeuvres

*You'll know I'm at the party if you see these salmon pin-wheels on the hors d'oeuvres platter. This is my perfect what-can-I-bring-along dish. The flatbread can be pur-chased at Arab or Lebanese specialty stores. Buy extra sheets and freeze until needed for the next party. They taste great and display beautifully.*

| | | |
|---|---|---|
| 1 | full sheet flatbread | 1 |
| 1 lb | light Quark cheese | 500 g |
| 6 oz | smoked salmon, thinly sliced | 184 g |
| 2 tbsp | pickled capers | 25 mL |
| 4 cups | shredded lettuce | 1L |
| 1 | medium tomato, diced | 1 |

Spread cheese evenly on flatbread. Distribute salmon slices over cheese. Top with capers, lettuce, and tomato. Firmly roll into a log and cover with plastic wrap to hold shape. Refrigerate at least 1 hour before serving.

SERVES 24

PER SERVING (1 slice)
*51 calories*
*1.6 g fat*
*18% of calories from fat*

## Stress

*What if all negative experiences in life could be eliminated, from major misfortunes such as divorce or the loss of a job to minor annoyances such as waiting in line or gaining a few pounds? Would life be free of stress? According to researchers at the University of California at Berkeley, the answer is no. They found that the presence of positive factors in life, rather than merely a lack of negative factors, was most important in reducing stress.*

*Balance everyday hassles with uplifts: pleasant, happy, satisfying experiences. Learn to recognize and enjoy them before they pass by. They will serve as buffers and insulators against life's negative experiences. Rejoice in the simple pleasures of life, and share your laughter and good deeds.*

# Soups

# Autumn Soup

*This soup looks and tastes like a cream soup but without the surplus calories and fat. It tastes better the next day, so refrigerate any leftovers and serve hot on chilly autumn days.*

| | | |
|---|---|---|
| 2 | medium, yellow crookneck squash, coarsely chopped | 2 |
| 1 | yellow or red bell pepper, seeded and chopped | 1 |
| 1 | large carrot, chopped | 1 |
| 1 tsp | curry powder | 5 mL |
| 1 tbsp | unsweetened orange juice concentrate | 15 mL |
| 2 cups | water | 500 mL |
| 1 | 10 oz (275 g) package frozen corn, thawed | 1 |
| 1 cup | skim milk | 250 mL |
| | hot pepper sauce to taste | |

■ Combine first six ingredients in a soup pot. Simmer, covered, for 30 minutes. Allow mixture to cool slightly. Transfer to a blender. Add corn and milk and puree until smooth. Return to soup pot and reheat; do not boil. Flavor with hot pepper sauce.

Serves 8

---

PER SERVING
*55 calories*
*0.2 g fat*
*3% calories from fat*

## Soup and Weight Loss

Souper news! Soup can play an influential role in weight loss programs.

While there is no such thing as foods that cause your body to get rid of fat, some foods can help limit the number of calories you consume. Soup is one of those foods. Researchers at the Institute of Behavioral Education in Pennsylvania found that eating soup at the beginning of a meal slows the rate of eating and fills the stomach, signaling the brain to reduce the appetite. Those who consumed soup four or more times each week lost an average of 20 percent of their excess weight.

If you'd like to incorporate soup into your weight loss program, stay away from cream soups. They average 13 grams of fat per serving. A broth-based soup is your best choice, and remember to skim the fat from the top before eating. I request an empty bowl in restaurants in order to do just that, especially if the soup has a shiny, oily surface.

## Fiber

If you love to eat—a lot—you've got to love fiber. It's become the nutritional buzzword of the 1990s, and the news about it just keeps getting better.

Besides being an integral part of weight control, we now know that fiber may play a significant role in reducing the risk of the leading chronic diseases: cancer, heart disease, and diabetes.

Fiber is actually a wide variety of substances with widely different properties, but what all fibers have in common is that they are the parts of plants that cannot be digested by enzymes in the human intestinal tract. There are two basic types of fiber. Insoluble fiber, found in wheat bran and whole grains, tends to move food quickly through the digestive tract and may protect against colon cancer. Soluble fiber, found primarily in beans, carrots, apples, and oranges, may lower blood cholesterol.

If your concern is weight loss, remember that high-fiber foods leave less room on your plate and in your stomach than high-fat foods such as meat and dairy products. The recommended daily intake of dietary fiber is at least 25 to 35 grams.

# Black Bean Soup

*A meal in itself with a powerhouse of fiber—beans. One cup (250 mL) of cooked beans has only 200 to 300 calories and 9 grams of fiber. This hearty version is ready in only 15 minutes.*

| | | |
|---|---|---|
| 1 | strip lean bacon, minced | 1 |
| 1 | medium carrot, finely chopped | 1 |
| 1 | celery stalk, finely chopped | 1 |
| ½ cup | onions, chopped | 125 mL |
| 3 | cloves garlic, crushed | 3 |
| 1 tsp | ground cumin | 5 mL |
| 3 | 16 oz (500 mL) cans black beans | 3 |
| 1 | medium tomato, cubed | 1 |
| 3 cups | defatted chicken broth, sodium reduced | 750 mL |
| ¼ cup | fresh cilantro, chopped | 50 mL |
| 1 tbsp | fresh lime juice | 15 mL |
| ¼ tsp | dried red chili pepper, crushed | 1 mL |
| ⅓ cup | nonfat sour cream | 75 mL |
| 2 tbsp | fresh parsley, chopped | 25 mL |

▦ Sauté bacon over medium heat for 3 to 5 minutes, or until golden. Add carrot, celery, onions, garlic, and cumin. Sauté for about 5 minutes, or until softened.

▦ Transfer mixture to a food processor. Add 2 cans undrained black beans and the tomato. Blend until very smooth and pour into a soup pot.

▦ Drain and rinse the remaining can of beans and add to the pot. Add chicken broth, cilantro, lime juice, and chili pepper. Heat and pour into bowls. Garnish with sour cream and parsley. Serve immediately.

SERVES 6

PER SERVING
*291 calories*
*4.6 g fat*
14% calories from fat

# Carrot Soup with Curry

*This recipe is from Mexico's Rancho La Puerta, where the fitness revolution began in 1940.*

| | | |
|---|---|---|
| 4 cups | vegetable stock (recipe below) | 1 L |
| 3 cups | carrots, peeled and sliced | 750 mL |
| ⅔ cup | onion, chopped | 150 mL |
| 2 tsp | fresh ginger, minced | 10 mL |
| 2 tsp | curry powder | 10 mL |
| 1 | garlic clove, minced | 1 |
| ½ cup | skim milk | 125 mL |
| 1 tsp | unsalted butter | 5 mL |
| | freshly ground white pepper | |
| 1 tbsp | fresh mint for garnish, chopped | 15 mL |

Combine vegetable stock, carrots, onion, ginger, curry, and garlic in a medium pot. Simmer, covered, for 35 minutes over low heat. Puree mixture in a blender until smooth. Return pureed soup to pot and add milk and butter. Season with white pepper. Bring soup to a boil. Serve in individual bowls with mint garnish.

### VEGETABLE STOCK (I)

| | | |
|---|---|---|
| 4 cups | unpeeled vegetables, cut into small pieces (leftovers are fine) | 1 L |
| 10 cups | water | 2.5 L |

In a saucepan prepared with nonstick cooking spray, sauté vegetables until tender. Place water in a stock pot and add the vegetables. Simmer slowly, about 1 ¼ hours, until reduced to half in volume. Strain and discard the vegetables. A good base for any soup, this stock has only 28 calories per cup (250 mL) and just a trace of fat.

SERVES 4

PER SERVING (I cup/250 mL)
*60 calories*
*I g fat*
*15% calories from fat*

# Beet and Buttermilk Soup

*Cool and refreshing, this summertime recipe is based on a soup I once had at the King Ranch Spa in Toronto.*

| | | |
|---|---|---|
| ¼ cup | nonfat sour cream | 50 mL |
| ¼ cup | low-fat cottage cheese | 50 mL |
| 2 cups | buttermilk | 500 mL |
| 2 | medium beets, cooked, peeled, cubed | 2 |
| ¼ | English cucumber, peeled, diced | ¼ |
| ¼ cup | fresh parsley, chopped | 50 mL |
| 1 | radish, slivered | 1 |
| 2 tbsp | fresh chives or scallions, chopped | 25 mL |
| | salt and freshly ground pepper | |

In blender or food processor, combine sour cream and cottage cheese. Process until smooth. Combine with buttermilk and refrigerate.

Just before serving, divide beets among serving bowls. Stir cucumber, parsley, radishes, and chives into buttermilk mixture. Season to taste with salt and pepper. Pour over beets.

SERVES 8

PER SERVING
*50 calories*
*1.5 g fat*
*27% calories from fat*

# Cream of Wild Mushroom Soup

*Executive chef Willie White of Edmonton's Hotel Macdonald skillfully prepared this rich tasting, low-fat soup for my spa program. The soup is so rich and creamy, it's hard to believe it contains no cream.*

| | | |
|---|---|---|
| ½ oz ea | dried morels and chanterelles | 15 g ea |
| | (or any other dried mushrooms) | 15 g |
| 3 cups | vegetable stock (recipe below) | 750 mL |
| 1 cup | onions, chopped | 250 mL |
| 2 tbsp | low-sodium soy sauce | 25 mL |
| ½ cup | field or button mushrooms, chopped | 125 mL |
| 1 tsp | sugar | 5 mL |
| ½ cup | whole wheat flour | 125 mL |
| ½ cup | water | 125 mL |
| 1 cup | buttermilk | 250 mL |
| ½ cup | evaporated skim milk paprika or fresh herbs for garnish | 125 mL |

■ Soak dried mushrooms in hot water until soft; clean and chop.

■ In a large saucepan, place mushrooms, stock, onions, soy sauce, and field mushrooms. Bring to a boil, then reduce heat to simmer.

■ In a separate bowl, combine sugar, whole wheat flour, and water. Mix into a smooth paste. Pour the paste through a sieve into the soup and mix thoroughly. Cook for 3 minutes, stirring occasionally.

■ Add buttermilk and skim milk and bring back to a simmer. Allow the soup to cool for 5 minutes. Puree in a blender. Return the soup to the saucepan and reheat slowly at a slight simmer. Serve sprinkled with paprika or fresh herbs.

### Weight Gain and Winter

*Does winter make you fat? Many people seem to gain weight more easily during the winter months. They also feel like curling up and sleeping right through the season. The hibernating process has always been attributed to the colder temperatures of winter, but actually it's the shorter days that's key. A substance called melatonin seems to trigger the onset of hibernation tendencies such as slowed activity and weight gain, a signal to store and conserve energy for the long, cold months ahead. A study on animals at the University of Aberdeen showed that animals exposed to fewer daylight hours had higher levels of melatonin. Scientists have discovered that humans react to reduced daylight hours with increased melatonin levels as well. We may not hibernate, but we do feel less energetic.*

*If you are trying to lose weight during the winter months, increase your metabolic rate. Regular exercise is essential for keeping off unwanted pounds and preventing winter blues. When you exercise, your body releases beta-endorphins, a natural high that may bring back those great summertime feelings, even in winter.*

## VEGETABLE STOCK (2)

| | | |
|---|---|---|
| ½ | leek, roots removed | ½ |
| 1 cup | parsnips, peeled | 250 mL |
| 1 cup | jumbo carrots, peeled | 250 mL |
| 1 | jumbo yellow onion, peeled | 1 |
| 1 | celery stalk | 1 |
| 6 | whole garlic cloves, peeled | 6 |
| 1 | small zucchini | 1 |
| 2 | medium tomatoes | 2 |
| ¼ | medium green cabbage | ¼ |
| 2 | broccoli florets | 2 |
| ½ | bunch parsley | ½ |
| 2 tbsp | fresh thyme | 25 mL |
| 2 tbsp | green basil | 25 mL |
| 2 | whole bay leaves | 2 |
| 1 tsp | whole black pepper | 5 mL |

To prepare stock, roughly chop the vegetables and parsley. Place in a stock pot and cover with 12 cups (3 L) of water. Bring to a boil over high heat. Add herbs and pepper. Reduce heat and simmer for 1 ½ hours. Strain stock and cool, then place in refrigerator. There are 28 calories per cup (250 mL) with just a trace of fat in this stock.

SERVES 4 GENEROUSLY

PER SERVING
*150 calories*
*1.2 g fat*
*7% calories from fat*

# Lentil Soup

*This soup tastes as good as it smells. With its practical, hearty ingredients, you can serve it with pride to family and friends.*

| | | |
|---|---|---|
| 3 cups | defatted chicken stock | 750 mL |
| ¼ cup | green lentils | 50 mL |
| ⅓ cup | red lentils | 75 mL |
| ½ cup | onions, diced | 125 mL |
| ⅓ cup | celery, diced | 75 mL |
| ⅓ cup | carrots, diced | 75 mL |
| ¼ cup | leeks, sliced | 50 mL |
| 1 | bay leaf | 1 |
| 1 tbsp | garlic, peeled and chopped | 15 mL |
| 2 tbsp | jalapeno pepper, diced | 25 mL |
| | salt and pepper to taste | |

Bring chicken stock to a boil. Add green lentils, reduce heat and cook, covered, for 1 hour. Add red lentils and cook for 30 minutes. Add remaining ingredients, except seasoning, and cook for another hour. Remove bay leaf.

In a blender, puree soup in batches. Return to pot and season with salt and pepper. Serve with whole-grain bread.

SERVES 8

PER SERVING
*70 calories*
*trace of fat*

# Spicy Corn Chowder

*This hearty corn chowder proves that comfort food does not have to be fattening food.*

| | | |
|---|---|---|
| 1 cup | onions, chopped | 250 mL |
| 2 tsp | canola oil | 10 mL |
| 1 | red bell pepper, seeded and diced | 1 |
| 1 | stalk celery, chopped | 1 |
| 2 | cloves garlic, crushed | 2 |
| 3 ½ cups | defatted chicken stock | 875 mL |
| 1 tsp | dried thyme | 5 mL |
| ½ tsp | dry mustard | 2 mL |
| 1 | bay leaf | 1 |
| 2 cups | corn kernels, fresh or frozen | 500 mL |
| 1 ½ cups | potato, peeled and diced | 375 mL |
| 1 ½ cups | evaporated skim milk | 375 mL |
| 2 tbsp | cornstarch | 25 mL |
| | freshly ground pepper | |
| | Tabasco sauce to taste | |

▇ Sauté onions in oil until translucent. Add red pepper, celery, and garlic. Sauté for 2 to 3 minutes. Add chicken stock, thyme, dry mustard, and bay leaf. Bring to a boil, then simmer on low heat, uncovered, for 10 minutes. Add corn and potatoes and simmer, covered, until vegetables are tender, about 5 to 10 minutes.

▇ In a small bowl, combine milk and cornstarch, stirring until smooth. Remove soup from heat. Slowly add milk mixture, stirring constantly. Return soup to a simmer and cook, stirring, for 2 minutes, or until thickened. Remove bay leaf. Season with pepper and Tabasco sauce.

SERVES 4

---

**PER SERVING**
*132 calories*
*2.5 g fat*
*17% calories from fat*

# Shrimp and Spinach Soup

*When I want something light and easy to prepare, this soup is just right. A hearty, whole-grain bread and green salad are all you need to turn this soup into a meal.*

| | | |
|---|---|---|
| 1 tsp | canola oil | 5 mL |
| ¾ cup | onion, chopped | 175 mL |
| 2 | celery sticks, chopped | 2 |
| 1 | small clove garlic, minced | 1 |
| ¼ tsp | dried red chili pepper, crushed | 1 mL |
| 1 | medium tomato, chopped | 1 |
| ¼ cup | basmati rice | 50 mL |
| 1 | 10 oz (284 mL) can defatted chicken broth | 1 |
| 1 ½ cups | water | 375 mL |
| ½ tsp | thyme | 2 mL |
| 1 ½ cup | thin strips spinach | 375 mL |
| 4 oz | shrimp, raw, peeled, deveined salt and freshly ground pepper | 125 g |

In a nonstick pan, heat oil over medium heat. Stir in onion, celery, garlic, and dried red chili pepper. Cover and cook until onions are tender, about 3 minutes. Add tomatoes, rice, chicken broth, water, and thyme. Cover and simmer for 35 minutes. Add spinach and shrimp and simmer another 5 minutes, or until rice is tender. Season to taste with salt and pepper.

SERVES 4

PER SERVING
*100 calories*
*2.5 g fat*
*23% calories from fat*

are included, nutrients such as thiamin, niacin, riboflavin, and iron are packed into the meal. The protein content can be boosted by adding legumes.

The memory of soup as a basic nourishment still lingers in the familiar cry of "Soup's on!" and fits in well with a health-promoting lifestyle.

# Salads

# Chow Mein Salad

*A popular dish served by many trendy restaurants, the revamped version here is just as good as the original, if not better.*

## SALAD

| | | |
|---|---|---|
| 8 oz | chicken breast, skinless, boneless (approximately 2 half breasts) | 250 g |
| 8 oz | shrimp, raw, peeled, deveined | 250 g |
| 1 ½ tsp | sesame oil | 7 mL |
| 3 tbsp | honey | 45 mL |
| 2 tbsp | soy sauce | 25 mL |
| 1 | 10 oz (284 mL) can mandarin oranges | |
| 1 | | |
| 6 cups | torn iceberg lettuce | 1.5 L |
| 1 cup | fresh bean sprouts | 250 mL |
| ½ cup | water chestnuts | 125 mL |
| 1 | bunch cilantro, chopped | 1 |
| 1 | red bell pepper, seeded, chopped | 1 |
| ¼ cup | avocado, diced | 50 mL |
| ¼ cup | cashews, chopped | 50 mL |
| ½ cup | chow mein noodles | 125 mL |

## DRESSING

| | | |
|---|---|---|
| ⅓ cup | seasoned rice vinegar | 75 mL |
| 1 | garlic clove, crushed | 1 |
| 1 tsp | fresh ginger, grated | 5 mL |
| 1 tsp | soy sauce | 5 mL |
| 1 tsp | sesame oil | 5 mL |

Cook chicken and shrimp. Slice chicken into strips.

Combine sesame oil, honey, and soy sauce. Drizzle over chicken and shrimp and marinate in refrigerator for 6 to 8 hours, or overnight if desired.

When ready to serve, drain mandarin oranges and toss with remaining salad ingredients.

Mix salad dressing ingredients together in a small

### Exercise—The Best Time

*Does it really matter what time
of day you exercise? Research
shows that when you exercise
can make a difference in the
effectiveness of your workout.
Although individual biorhythms
vary, strength peaks at noon for
most people while aerobic and
anaerobic capacity are at their
highest in the afternoon. According to Dave Hill, Assistant Pro-
fessor of Kinesiology at the University of North Texas, both
muscle strength and aerobic
potential are at their peak
around four in the afternoon.*

*Before you reset your alarm
clock and switch your exercise
schedule, consider that morning
exercise has its benefits, too. A
study of exercisers at William
Beaumont Hospital in Michigan
revealed that morning exercisers are more likely to stick to
their programs. Leaving exercise
until the end of the day allows
excuses to pile up as the day
goes on.*

*Whether you exercise morn-
ing, afternoon, or evening, the
best time of day is when you
are most likely to do it. Along
with proper nutrition, a consistent exercise program is an
integral part of weight control.*

bowl. Toss salad with dressing and divide salad equally
among plates. Top with glazed chicken and shrimp.

SERVES 4

___

**PER SERVING**
*390 calories*
*11 g fat*
*25% calories from fat*

# Strawberry Spinach Salad

*This slightly sweet and savory dressing is perfect for a simple salad of spinach and strawberries. Use your imagination and substitute strawberries with fresh, ripened peaches or raspberries if you like.*

### SALAD

| ½ lb | fresh spinach | 250 g |
| 2 cups | fresh strawberries, sliced | 500 mL |

### DRESSING

| 2 tbsp | plain low-fat yogurt | 25 mL |
| 3 tbsp | reduced-calorie mayonnaise | 45 mL |
| ¼ cup | unsweetened orange juice | 50 mL |
| 1 tsp | sugar | 5 mL |

▣ To prepare spinach, wash leaves thoroughly under cold running water. Pat dry on paper towels and trim off tough stems and ribs, as necessary. Gently toss spinach and sliced strawberries in a large bowl. Arrange on individual salad plates.

▣ Combine dressing ingredients in a small bowl and stir well. Drizzle mixture over each salad.

SERVES 8

PER SERVING
*54 calories*
*2.7 g*
*45% calories from fat*

## Undereating

Do you eat a second meal while cleaning the kitchen after dinner? I cured myself of that habit years ago when I unknowingly licked the spoon used to dish out the dog food. It was no wonder anything on a spoon looked good. I had just finished another day of strict dieting.

Starving in an attempt to lose weight is not recommended. It will lead to overeating, and depriving yourself of food will not result in permanent weight loss. The weight you lose will be primarily fluids and quickly regained.

Fortunately, you do not have to feel hungry all the time to lose weight. A recent study cited in the American Journal of Clinical Nutrition suggests you only need to reduce fat intake to successfully and painlessly lose weight. Study participants were told to eat as much and as often as they wished. Their only requirement was to limit total fat intake to less than 25 percent of their daily calories. After eleven weeks, they lost an average of six pounds each. The good news is they never suffered hunger pangs.

# Primavera Pasta Salad

*A terrific summer dish and a tasty accompaniment to grilled fish or chicken.*

## SALAD

| | | |
|---|---|---|
| 8 oz | rotini or spiral pasta | 250 g |
| ½ cup | frozen peas, thawed | 125 mL |
| 1 | medium red onion, sliced | 1 |
| 12 oz | fresh or frozen asparagus, cut into ½-inch (1 cm) pieces | 350 g |
| 1 cup | fresh mushrooms, thinly sliced | 250 mL |
| 1 cup | carrots, thinly sliced | 250 mL |
| 4 | large lettuce leaves | 4 |

## DRESSING

| | | |
|---|---|---|
| 1 tbsp | olive oil | 15 mL |
| ⅓ cup | defatted chicken broth | 75 mL |
| 3 tbsp | balsamic vinegar | 45 mL |
| 3 | cloves garlic, crushed | 3 |
| ½ tsp | dried red chili pepper, crushed | 2 mL |
| 2 tbsp | Parmesan cheese, grated | 25 mL |
| ½ cup | sun-dried tomatoes, diced | 125 mL |

▪ Combine dressing ingredients and set aside for at least 1 hour.

▪ Cook pasta according to package directions. Drain. Stir in peas, onion, mushrooms, and carrots. Cook asparagus for 1 minute, or according to package directions if frozen. Drain and add to pasta.

▪ Add dressing to pasta mixture and mix well. Line salad plates with lettuce leaves, add salad, and serve.

SERVES 4

PER SERVING
*336 calories*
*6.5 g fat*
*17% calories from fat*

# Soba Noodle Salad

*While most people think of rice when they think of Japanese food, the Japanese are in fact great noodle eaters. Rice and noodles are diametrically opposed in Japanese cuisine. Rice is eaten with deep reverence, unblemished by condiments. Noodles, on the other hand, are almost always souped or sauced, and they are noisily slurped. To eat noodles quietly is considered insulting. The soba noodles in this salad are made from buckwheat and have a coarse texture and nutty taste. If you want a change from the same old salads, be adventuresome and try this one. Who says low-fat eating has to be dull!*

## SALAD

| | | |
|---|---|---|
| 6 | fresh shitake mushrooms, sliced | 6 |
| ¼ cup | defatted chicken broth | 50 mL |
| 4 cups | broccoli florets | 1 L |
| 2 | red bell peppers | 2 |
| 8 oz | soba noodles | 250 g |
| | lettuce leaves | |

## HERB VINAIGRETTE

| | | |
|---|---|---|
| 2 tbsp | cider vinegar | 25 mL |
| 2 tsp | sesame oil | 10 mL |
| 1 tsp | fresh ginger, minced | 5 mL |
| 1 | small clove garlic, minced | 1 |
| 1 tbsp | parsley, chopped | 15 mL |
| 1 tbsp | fresh herbs, chopped (basil, thyme, tarragon, chives, cilantro) | 15 mL |
| | pinch sugar | |
| | salt and pepper | |

Sauté mushrooms in chicken broth over medium heat until tender. Blanch broccoli in boiling water for 2 minutes. Drain and rinse under cold water. Drain again.

Roast peppers over gas flame or grill for 10 minutes,

## THE DIET-CANCER Connection

Once upon a time when life was simple, there were no suspicions that perils lurked unrecognized on the dinner table.

Now, hardly a week passes without alarming new claims about possible links between food and cancer. Researchers now believe that diet may be the precipitating factor in up to 30 percent of cancer deaths. Diet, like smoking, may be one of the few risk factors over which we have direct control.

Although the diet-cancer relationship is hotly debated among medical scientists, data strongly suggests that a low-fat, high-fiber diet rich in fruits and vegetables may help prevent cancer. Dr. Brian Henderson, director of the Kenneth Norris Comprehensive Cancer Center at the University of California, indicates that there is a reasonably well-established relationship between saturated fat and colon and rectal cancer. A 1990 study by Dr. Geoffrey Howe of the National Cancer Institute singled out dietary fat as a possible culprit in breast cancer. He suggests that if all North American women lower their saturated fat intake, breast cancer cases among postmenopausal women would fall about 10 percent. Adding vitamin C-rich produce to the diet would cut cases an additional 16 percent. Scientists have shown that dietary fiber may also reduce the risk of breast cancer, per-

*haps by influencing the body's metabolism of estrogen.*

*The National Cancer Institute has come up with a list of eight cancer-fighting foods and food elements: fiber, cruciferous vegetables, vitamin C, beta-carotene, Omega-3 fatty acids, vitamin E, folic acid, and selenium. Until the links between diet and disease prevention (and perhaps even cure) are clearly established, many doctors agree that these dietary factors can do no harm and may even help.*

or in 450 F (230 C) oven for 20 minutes. Peppers should be soft with skin blackened slightly and blistered. Place in plastic bag, seal and let peppers steam for 10 minutes. Scrape skin from peppers, discard seeds, and cut into strips.

■ In a large pot of boiling water, cook noodles until tender yet firm, about 10 minutes. Drain and rinse under cold water. Drain again.

■ Combine vinaigrette ingredients in a small bowl and mix well.

■ In a salad bowl, combine noodles, mushrooms, broccoli, peppers, and vinaigrette. Toss to mix and serve on lettuce-lined plates.

SERVES 4

---

PER SERVING
*170 calories*
*5 grams fat*
*26% calories from fat*

# Lentil Salad with Fennel

*This tasty, wilt-proof salad is perfect for picnics or buffets.*

## SALAD

| | | |
|---|---|---|
| 1 cup | brown lentils | 250 mL |
| ½ cup | shallots, sliced | 125 mL |
| 1 | carrot, thinly sliced on diagonal | 1 |
| ½ cup | fennel, chopped | 125 mL |
| 1 tsp | cumin | 5 mL |
| 2 tbsp | water | 25 mL |
| ¼ cup | Italian parsley, chopped, packed | 50 mL |
| ¼ cup | green onion, minced | 50 mL |
| 2 tbsp | green chilis, canned or roasted, chopped | 25 mL |
| 1 cup | cucumber, unpeeled, diced | 250 mL |

## DRESSING

| | | |
|---|---|---|
| 2 tbsp | white wine vinegar | 25 mL |
| 1 tsp | olive oil | 5 mL |
| 1 tsp | warm water | 5 mL |
| | salt and pepper to taste | |

▪ In a large pot of boiling water, cook lentils for 20 minutes, or until tender. Drain. In a nonstick frying pan, sauté shallots, carrot, fennel, and cumin in 2 tbsp (25 mL) water, covered, for 5 minutes, or until tender. Uncover and cook until liquid evaporates.

▪ Combine lentils, carrot mixture, parsley, onion, chili, and cucumber in a salad bowl.

▪ In another small bowl, combine vinegar, oil, and water and mix well. Pour over salad and toss to mix. Add salt and pepper to taste.

SERVES 6

**PER SERVING**
*67 calories*
*trace of fat*

Tighten your belt as well as your purse strings by buying food that is nutritious. Healthy food generally costs less than a dollar per pound and includes rice, pasta, whole wheat flour, dried beans and legumes, potatoes, carrots, bananas, and seasonal fruits and vegetables. Dairy products and meats cost more, but the amounts needed don't make up the major portion of a healthy diet. Processed foods are expensive and quite often fattening because the fat cannot be skimmed or trimmed away.

A recent study conducted by Cornell University indicates that women in mid- to high-income levels eat proportionately more fruits, vegetables, and high-fiber breads and cereals than lower-income women. Those with incomes near or below the poverty level consume fat the traditional way through luncheon meats, bacon, processed snacks, and whole milk. Overall, who eats more fat? The higher-income group. They sabotage their good efforts with expensive baked goods and cheeses. However, it's possible for everyone to eat a lower fat diet. What's important is nutrition education.

# Salad Dressings

*Too often, the most nutritious, low-calorie salad is spoiled by an oily, high-calorie dressing. A classic vinaigrette with its three-to-one oil-to-vinegar ratio yields 10 grams of fat and 90 calories per tablespoon. That so-called healthy salad can cost you about 30 grams of fat and 300 calories before you've even seen the main course. If you're going to splurge, why not blow your fat budget on a sinful dessert instead of a salad! A few tricks and substitutes can create great salad dressings that are low in fat, calories, and sodium.*

*The following salad dressings are favorites of mine and my guests at the health spas I conduct. The dressings can be made ahead and kept in the refrigerator for up to three days. Each recipe makes approximately 1 cup (250 mL).*

*Choose a selection of greens such as leaf lettuce, spinach, watercress, endive and basil, add a variety of fresh, raw vegetables, and toss with any one of these sumptuous dressings.*

# Roasted Garlic Dressing

| 2 | heads garlic | 2 |
| ½ cup | defatted chicken stock | 125 mL |
| ¼ cup | wine or cider vinegar | 50 mL |
| 2 tbsp | olive oil | 25 mL |
| 2 tsp | Dijon mustard | 10 mL |
| | salt and pepper to taste | |

Preheat oven to 400 F (200 C).

Remove the loose, papery skin from the garlic head without separating the cloves. Slice off ¼ inch (.5 cm) from the top of the head and discard. Wrap the garlic head in aluminum foil and roast for approximately 45 minutes, or until the garlic is very soft. Unwrap and cool enough to separate the cloves and peel.

In a food processor or blender, combine garlic cloves, chicken stock, oil, vinegar, and mustard. Blend until smooth. Season with salt and pepper. Dressing can be stored in an airtight container in the refrigerator for up to 2 days.

PER SERVING (1 tbsp/15 mL)
*32 calories*
*3 g fat*
*84% calories from fat*

## Garlic's Curative Power

*Garlic, a member of the onion family, has for centuries been considered the proverbial cure-all, the poor man's penicillin. Garlic's preventive and curative qualities have long been the subject of scientific investigation. It contains a substance which interferes with the formation of blood clots, may help reduce cholesterol, and some researchers suggest that garlic may have anticancer properties.*

*To select top-grade garlic, choose the whitest garlic you can find. Garlic is harvested in the summer and whiteness indicates freshness. Pick large, plump, firm bulbs with a tight sheath and store in a cool, ventilated place. It is generally impossible to find white garlic between January and May.*

## The Diet Industry

*Promises! Promises! Power come-ons from the $33 billion diet industry are hard to resist. "You can lose ten pounds in two weeks, be three sizes trimmer in just three weeks!" Commercial weight loss clinics are forced into flamboyant advertising practices in order to compete in the industry. They have to outdo each other to attract clients. And yes, pounds do drop fast in the first week of any diet, but the loss is water, not fat.*

*If you're looking for group support, commercial weight loss clinics are a reasonable choice. But while you can buy support from weight loss clinics, what you can't buy is a fast and miraculous way to lose weight.*

*The leading liquid diet plans offered through doctors and hospitals forego food altogether. Patients drink formula for twelve to sixteen weeks, and then add a low-calorie meal to the regimen until they reach their goal weight. Typically, an obese dieter can lose up to ten pounds the first week and three to five pounds each subsequent week. In the best programs, rapid weight loss is followed by counseling and medical checkups. Dr. Thomas Wadden, an obesity researcher at the University of Pennsylvania, found that dieters on medically supervised, low-calorie diets regain 25 to 60 percent of their weight within the first*

# Roasted Red Pepper Vinaigrette

| 2 | medium red bell peppers | 2 |
| 2 tbsp | shallots, chopped | 25 mL |
| 2 tbsp | balsamic vinegar | 25 mL |
| | salt and pepper to taste | |

■ Grill red peppers over barbecue or gas flame for about 15 minutes, turning until skin is blackened all over, or place on a baking sheet in oven at 375 F (190 C) for 30 minutes, turning once or twice until skin is blackened. Place in a plastic bag, seal and cool for 10 minutes, then peel and seed.

■ In a small saucepan over medium heat, cook shallots and vinegar, covered tightly, for 2 minutes, or until shallots are tender. Puree in a blender with roasted pepper. Add salt and pepper to taste.

---

**PER SERVING (2 tbsp/25 mL)**
*8 calories*
*trace of fat*

---

# *Tarragon Dressing*

| | | |
|---|---|---|
| ½ cup | red wine vinegar | 125 mL |
| 1 tbsp | sugar | 15 mL |
| 2 | garlic cloves, minced | 2 |
| | – OR – | |
| ½ tsp | garlic powder | 2 mL |
| 2 tsp | Worcestershire sauce | 10 mL |
| 1 tbsp | Dijon mustard | 15 mL |
| | juice of ½ lemon | |
| 1 ½ tbsp | olive oil | 20 mL |
| 1 cup | water | 250 mL |
| ¾ tsp | salt | 4 mL |
| 1 tbsp | dried tarragon | 15 mL |
| ¼ tsp | freshly ground pepper | 1 mL |

Mix all ingredients together in a blender. Refrigerate.

PER SERVING (2 tbsp/25 mL)
20 calories
1.6 g
72% calories from fat

year. After five years, on average, all the weight has returned.

If you want to try losing weight on your own, keep your calorie intake above 1,200 calories a day. More restrictive diets slow metabolism too much. Avoid fat as much as possible. Fat has over twice as many calories as carbohydrates and protein and loves to settle in the body's fat cells, which, of course, happen to be in all the wrong places. Make exercise a part of your lifestyle. Forever.

Commercial weight loss programs or formula diets that acknowledge these realities can still be reasonable options.

## Body Image

*How good you look is how good you are. Right or wrong, this idea is indicative of society's attitude toward weight and self-worth. By equating a good life with a certain body shape, you put your life on hold until you reach your perceived ideal weight. You feel you don't deserve to buy new clothes or take that dream vacation until you are thinner. The longer you remain overweight, the further you push your dreams into the future.*

*By learning to resist social pressure to meet unattainable standards, you can set goals that are within your reach. You cannot change your shape completely because body fat distribution is highly inherited. (If you have a pear-shaped body and lose weight, you will have a leaner pear shape.) And not everyone can look like a fashion model. What you are capable of, however, is a well-defined, healthy body maintained through exercise and proper nutrition. It's a goal that can be achieved by everyone.*

# Goat Cheese Dressing

| | | |
|---|---|---|
| 3 tbsp | goat cheese | 45 mL |
| ⅔ cup | buttermilk | 150 mL |
| 1 tsp | cider or sherry vinegar | 5 mL |
| ¼ tsp | minced garlic | 1 mL |
| | freshly ground pepper | |

■ In a blender, combine cheese, milk, vinegar, garlic, and pepper to taste. Blend until smooth. Cover and refrigerate up to 5 days.

---

PER SERVING (1 1/2 tbsp /20 mL)
*18 calories*
*1 gram fat*
*50% calories from fat*

---

# Spa Vinaigrette

| | | |
|---|---|---|
| 1 tbsp | Dijon mustard | 15 mL |
| 2 tbsp | extra-virgin olive oil | 25 mL |
| 2 tbsp | defatted chicken stock | 25 mL |
| 2 tbsp | red wine vinegar | 25 mL |
| 1 tbsp | shallots | 15 mL |
| 1 ½ tsp | lime juice | 7 mL |
| 1 tbsp | chives | 15 mL |
| | freshly ground white pepper to taste | |
| | lemon pepper seasoning to taste | |

▪ Put mustard in a small bowl and whisk in oil slowly. Whisk in the remaining ingredients. Add pepper and seasoning to taste. This will keep in a tightly covered container for 1 week.

PER SERVING (1 tbsp/15 mL)
*30 calories*
*2.4 g fat*
*72% calories from fat*

# Vegetables

# Spinach Phyllo Casserole

*The layers of this low-fat phyllo pastry are coated with a mixture of egg whites and olive oil instead of melted butter.*

| ¼ cup | onion, chopped | 50 mL |
|---|---|---|
| ¼ cup | defatted chicken broth | 50 mL |
| 2 tbsp | all-purpose flour | 25 mL |
| ½ cup | skim milk | 125 mL |
| 8 oz | low-fat Cheddar cheese, grated | 250 g |
| 10 oz | fresh or frozen spinach, cooked, drained and chopped | 275 g |
| 7 | egg whites | 7 |
| 3 | sheets phyllo pastry | 3 |
| 2 tbsp | olive oil | 25 mL |

Preheat oven to 375 F (190 C).

Sauté onions in chicken broth until broth has evaporated.

Stir flour into milk until dissolved. Add to onions and stir constantly over medium heat until thickened. Blend in cheese until melted.

Remove from heat and stir in spinach. Beat 6 egg whites until frothy and blend into cheese mixture. Pour into a deep casserole dish brushed with olive oil.

Whisk together remaining egg white and the olive oil. Blend well. Cut sheets of phyllo pastry in half. Top the casserole with one piece of phyllo pastry. Brush with egg white mixture. Continue layering phyllo sheets, brushing each with the mixture. Bake for 35 to 45 minutes.

SERVES 8

PER SERVING
*149 calories*
*5.1 g fat*
*22% calories from fat.*

## Eat More and Weigh Less

*Trying to lose a few pounds? Try eating more. More of the right kinds of food. In fact, if you switch to low-fat eating, you can eat a lot more than you might imagine. One explanation is that the brain, liver, sections of the spinal cord, and gastrointestinal tract contain receptors that keep track of carbohydrates eaten. This is important because carbohydrates are broken down into glucose, a quick and important source of energy. When you reduce carbohydrates in your diet, your body tries to restore the deficit by stimulating your appetite. Since fat receptors don't exist, your body doesn't complain when you limit your fat intake.*

*Reducing fat also reduces calories. One fat gram contains 9 calories; carbohydrates and protein contain 4 calories. Example: You would have to eat 221 pretzel sticks before you'd equal the 420 calories in a handful of peanuts. Because pretzels contain very little fat, you would have to eat a mountain of them before you could match the mega load of fat, approximately 60 grams, in the handful of peanuts. The great thing about low-fat eating is that you will never go hungry.*

# Vegetables and Couscous

| | | |
|---|---|---|
| 1 ⅓ cups | dried chick peas | 325 mL |
| 4 cups | fresh plum tomatoes, quartered | 1 L |
| 1 ½ cups | sweet potato, peeled and cubed | 375 mL |
| 4 | medium carrots, cut in chunks | 4 |
| 1 ½ cups | parsnips, peeled and cubed | 375 mL |
| 1 cup | chopped onion | 250 mL |
| 1 cup | cabbage, coarsely chopped | 250 mL |
| 1 cup | mushrooms, stems removed, coarsely chopped | 250 mL |
| ¼ cup | Italian parsley, coarsely chopped | 50 mL |
| 2 tsp | garlic, minced | 10 mL |
| 1 tsp | saffron threads | 5 mL |
| 1 cup | water | 250 mL |
| 2 cups | broccoli florets | 500 mL |
| | salt and pepper | |
| 1 ½ cups | couscous | 375 mL |

In a large pot, bring 4 cups (1 L) of water to a boil. Add chick peas, cook gently for 2 minutes. Remove from heat, let stand approximately 1 hour, covered, then drain.

In a large saucepan, combine cooked chick peas with remaining ingredients except broccoli. Bring to a boil, reduce heat, cover and simmer for 30 minutes, or until vegetables are tender. Add broccoli and cook another 5 minutes, or until broccoli is crisp-tender. Season with salt and pepper to taste.

Prepare couscous (see below) and serve with vegetables.

SERVES 8

---

PER SERVING (1 cup/250 mL with couscous)
*200 calories*
*2 grams fat*
*9% calories from fat*

# Couscous

*Couscous is available at some supermarkets and most health food stores. If buying packaged couscous, follow directions on package. If buying in bulk, use the directions below.*

| 1 ½ cups | precooked couscous | 375 mL |
| 2 cups | water | 500 mL |

Bring water to a boil and add couscous. Cover and let stand for 5 minutes. Fluff with a fork.

SERVES 8

---

PER SERVING (1/2 cup/125 mL)
*101 calories*
*0.4 grams fat*
*3.6% calories from fat*

---

## The Truth About Potatoes

*If you love potatoes but have abandoned your relationship with the humble spud because you think it's fattening, you can renew your romance. Here is the ungarnished truth about potatoes. One large, baked potato with skin has about 220 calories and less than a gram of fat, lots of vitamin C, a generous amount of B vitamins, potassium, iron, a fair amount of fiber, and some protein. Add butter, cream, mayonnaise, or oil, and this nutritional bargain is devalued. Top your potato instead with low-fat cottage cheese, yogurt, or sour cream, or try salsa or Dijon mustard for a kick.*

# Scalloped Potatoes

*The potatoes in this recipe are steamed in skim milk, topped with a layer of low-fat sour cream, and broiled until golden brown. The results are anything but boring.*

| | | |
|---|---|---|
| 4 cups | potatoes, peeled and thinly sliced (about 3 medium) | 1 L |
| 1 | onion, thinly sliced | 1 |
| 3 | cloves garlic, crushed | 3 |
| 2 cups | skim milk | 500 mL |
| ½ tsp | salt | 2 mL |
| | freshly ground pepper to taste | |
| ¼ cup | low-fat sour cream | 50 mL |
| ¼ cup | plain low-fat yogurt | 50 mL |
| 2 tbsp | Parmesan cheese, grated | 25 mL |

▦ Spray an 11 x 8 x 2-inch (28 x 20 x 5 cm) casserole dish with nonstick cooking spray.

▦ In a medium-size, heavy saucepan, combine potatoes, onions, garlic, milk, salt, and pepper. Simmer over low heat, uncovered, until potatoes are tender, about 10 minutes. Using a slotted spoon, transfer potatoes to the casserole dish.

▦ Combine sour cream and yogurt. Measure out ¼ cup (50 mL) of the milk mixture from the casserole dish and add to sour cream and yogurt.

▦ Preheat broiler. Spoon the sour cream-yogurt mixture evenly over the potatoes. Sprinkle with Parmesan cheese and broil until golden brown. Serve immediately.

SERVES 4

PER SERVING
*196 calories*
*3.8 g fat*
*18% calories from fat*

# Marinated Wild Mushrooms

*I never met a mushroom I didn't like. Mushrooms are so low in calories, approximately 40 per cup (250 mL), that you practically burn up those calories just eating them. Whether served hot or cold, this recipe is terrific as a side dish, especially with grilled, lean steak.*

| | | |
|---|---|---|
| 5 | cloves garlic, peeled and minced | 5 |
| 3 | sprigs fresh rosemary, chopped <br> – OR – | 3 |
| ½ tsp | dried rosemary | 2 mL |
| 4 sprigs ea | fresh thyme and parsley, chopped <br> – OR – | 4 sprigs ea |
| ½ tsp ea | dried thyme and parsley | 2 mL ea |
| ½ cup | balsamic vinegar | 125 mL |
| 4 cups | water | 1 L |
| 1 ½ lb | fresh mushrooms (combination of portabello, oyster, shitake and plain) salt and pepper to taste | 750 g |

In a saucepan, combine garlic, herbs, vinegar, and water. Bring to a boil, then simmer, covered, for 10 minutes.

Add mushrooms and simmer for 2 minutes, or until mushrooms begin to shrink and are tender. Remove mushrooms with a slotted spoon and set aside.

Return liquid to saucepan and boil until reduced to ½ cup (125 mL). Set aside to cool. When cool, pour over mushrooms and season to taste.

SERVES 8

PER SERVING
*43 calories*
*0 g fat*

## Handling Potatoes

*Potatoes contain a certain amount of solanine concentrated mostly in the skin and sprouts. When bruised, subjected to bright light or extreme temperatures, or just kept around too long, potatoes produce even more solanine which could make you ill if eaten in large quantities. It's been suggested that cooking potatoes with their skins may cause solanine to migrate from the skin into the flesh of the potato; however, the general consensus from most researchers is that the skin is by far the most nutritious part of the potato. If you avoid potatoes that are obviously in bad shape, pare away any green areas, and gouge out any sprouts, potatoes are safe to eat. If a cooked potato tastes bitter, it may contain significant amounts of solanine so don't eat it.*

# Cheese-Stuffed Potatoes

*Try these cheese-stuffed potatoes next time you're entertaining. Prepare them ahead of time and heat just before serving.*

| | | |
|---|---|---|
| 5 | large baking potatoes | 5 |
| 1 cup | plain low-fat yogurt | 250 mL |
| 2 cups | low-fat cottage cheese | 500 mL |
| 1 cup | low-fat Cheddar cheese, grated | 250 mL |
| 2 tbsp | green onions, finely chopped | 25 mL |
| 1 tbsp | fresh parsley, chopped | 15 mL |
| | salt and pepper | |
| ¼ cup | Parmesan cheese, grated (optional) | 50 mL |

Preheat oven to 375 F (190 C).

Bake potatoes for 1 hour, or until done. Slice potatoes in half lengthwise and scoop out centers. Place potato shells aside.

In a food processor, blend together the potatoes, yogurt, and cottage cheese until smooth. Add Cheddar cheese, onion, and parsley. Season to taste.

Fill each potato shell with potato mixture and top with Parmesan cheese. Bake until hot, approximately 10 minutes.

SERVES 10

---

**PER SERVING**
*202 calories*
*2.8 g fat*
*12% calories from fat*

# Vegetarian Deli Sandwich

*This delicious vegetarian sandwich is a satisfying midday meal.*

| | | |
|---|---|---|
| 1 | French breadstick, 6-inches long (15 cm) (or a Kaiser bun) | 1 |
| 1 tsp | olive oil | 5 mL |
| 1 tsp | nonfat Italian dressing | 5 mL |
| 1 | thin slice, skim mozzarella cheese | 1 |
| ½ | medium tomato, sliced | ½ |
| ¼ | medium red or green bell pepper, sliced | ¼ |
| 6 | thin slices cucumber | 6 |
| ⅓ cup | alfalfa sprouts | 75 g |

▣ Slice French breadstick or Kaiser bun horizontally. Mix olive oil with dressing and brush evenly over inside of bread. To assemble sandwich, layer cheese, tomato, pepper, cucumber, and sprouts between bread.

SERVES 1

---

PER SERVING (1 sandwich)
*345 calories*
*11 g fat*
*28% calories from fat*

---

## Dangerous Delis

Many of us turn to the supermarket deli counter for sustenance, but beware. Evil may lurk in those takeout Styrofoam containers. Not only is the price of convenience food exorbitant, but you may also be paying for convenience with your health.

The danger of the deli counter is twofold. First, even when you intend to buy only the most healthful items, you can't always tell what you're getting. Since there are no labels, there is nothing to indicate that the product may be loaded with fat—which is really kind of nice. It allows you to eat with less guilt. Second, those good intentions to eat healthy are inclined to wither the longer you stare at the display in your hungry state. There it is, all the food staring back. All you have to do is point and it's yours.

My favorite part of deli shopping is asking questions about the food. You'd think from all the activity going on behind the counter that the salespeople are actually involved in the creation of the food. Wrong! What they are really doing is combining Package A and Sauce B with Garnish C, so when you ask a question the response is "I don't know. Would you like a taste?" I don't necessarily learn a lot about the food, but if I ask enough questions I can have an inexpensive, multicourse meal on the spot.

Of course, there is certainly

no reason to avoid the supermarket deli completely, provided you exercise good judgment. Don't buy more food than you can eat at one sitting. Forego anything with lots of cheese, rich sauces, mayonnaise, sour cream, or butter; in other words, anything that shines. Choose simple dishes. The less elaborate the recipe, the less likely it will contain unwholesome ingredients. So why not buy the three or four ingredients necessary to prepare it yourself and save a few dollars? I, for one, would miss the nice people behind the counter.

# Sweet Potato Soufflé

*My father refused to eat yams because that was what he fed his livestock as a boy growing up on a farm in the Ukraine. The lowly sweet potato has achieved higher status in North America and is even served in the finest of restaurants. Give your yam an attitude and dress it up in a soufflé.*

| | | |
|---|---|---|
| ½ lb | sweet potato or yam, peeled and thinly sliced (approximately 2 medium or 1 large) | 250 g |
| ¾ cup | orange juice | 175 mL |
| 1 cup | water | 250 mL |
| 1 tbsp | honey | 15 mL |
| 1 tsp | vanilla extract | 5 mL |
| ½ tsp | cinnamon | 2 mL |
| ⅛ tsp | nutmeg | .5 mL |
| 2 | large egg whites | 2 |
| | large pinch cream of tartar | |

■ Preheat oven to 400 F (200 C). Lightly coat four ½ cup (125 mL) soufflé baking dishes with nonstick cooking spray.

■ Combine sweet potato slices, orange juice, and water in a medium saucepan and bring to a boil. Reduce heat and cover. Cook potatoes until very soft, about 35 minutes. A small amount of water may be added to the mixture if the liquid evaporates before the potatoes are soft. Drain any extra liquid.

■ Spoon potatoes into a blender or food processor. Add honey, vanilla, cinnamon, and nutmeg. Puree the mixture until smooth and transfer to a medium bowl.

■ Beat the egg whites and cream of tartar together until soft peaks form. Fold half the egg whites into the potato mixture until mixture is lighter in color. Fold in remaining egg whites.

Spoon ½ cup (125 mL) of soufflé mixture into each soufflé baking dish. Bake for 25 minutes, or until fluffy and golden.

SERVES 4

**PER SERVING**
*75 calories*
*trace of fat*

## *Polenta*

*Polenta is a fun alternative to potatoes, rice, or pasta. It is an Old World dish that is economical and easy to make.*

| | | |
|---|---|---|
| 2 cups | water or stock | 500 mL |
| 1 tbsp | soy sauce | 15 mL |
| 1 cup | coarse cornmeal | 250 mL |
| 2 tbsp | Parmesan cheese | 25 mL |

▢ Bring water to a boil. Slowly add cornmeal in a steady stream, stirring constantly to avoid lumps. Add soy sauce and cheese. Lower heat and simmer slowly for 10 minutes. Turn heat off and let cool slightly.

▢ Pour into a pie plate lightly sprayed with nonstick cooking spray. Let polenta dry for a few hours. Bake at 400 F (200 C) for about 20 to 30 minutes. Serve hot.

SERVES 8

PER SERVING (1 wedge)
*150 calories*
*1.3 g fat*
*8% calories from fat*

# Vegetable Omelet

*This fluffy, delicate omelet leaves plenty of room for toasted English muffins or other favorite breakfast treats. It's a perfect way to start the weekend or a comforting way to end it, whenever you are looking for something light to eat.*

| ½ cup | mushrooms, sliced | 125 mL |
| ½ cup | zucchini, finely chopped | 125 mL |
| ¼ cup | green onions, chopped | 50 mL |
| ¼ cup | tomato, chopped | 50 mL |
| | dash of pepper | |
| 2 | egg whites | 2 |
| ¾ cup | frozen egg substitute, thawed | 175 mL |
| 2 tbsp | skim milk | 25 mL |
| ¼ tsp | dried parsley | 1 mL |
| ¼ tsp | dried cilantro | 1 mL |
| | salt and pepper to taste | |
| ¼ cup | low-fat Cheddar cheese, shredded | 50 mL |

Coat a 6-inch (15 cm) frying pan with nonstick cooking spray. Heat over medium heat until hot.

Add mushrooms, zucchini, onions, and tomato. Sauté 2 to 3 minutes, or until tender. Stir in a dash of pepper. Remove from frying pan and set aside. Keep warm.

Make sure egg whites are at room temperature. Beat until egg whites are stiff but not dry and set aside. Combine egg substitute and remaining ingredients in a separate bowl and stir well. Gently fold egg whites into egg substitute mixture.

Coat a frying pan with nonstick cooking spray. Place over medium heat until hot enough to sizzle a drop of water. Spread half the egg mixture in frying pan. Cover and reduce heat to low. Cook for 5 minutes, or until fluffy and golden brown on the bottom, gently lifting omelet edge to judge color. Cook omelet on other side for an additional 3 minutes.

## A Good Egg?

*Once called the perfect food, the egg, somewhat unfairly, has gained a reputation as the worst food to send cholesterol levels soaring. As a result, consumption has dropped. Most nutrition experts now agree that 4 whole eggs per week, cholesterol and all, fit well into the bounds of a healthy diet. Reducing the saturated fat in your diet, even more than reducing cholesterol, is the key to reducing blood cholesterol. Eggs, though high in cholesterol, are low in saturated fat (about 1.6 grams per large egg). If you partake of a diet that is mostly vegetarian and contains only low-fat dairy products, you can eat more than the recommended number of eggs per week.*

*If you're looking to reduce cholesterol, it's as simple as it's cracked up to be. Substituting 1 egg with 2 egg whites will not affect the outcome of the finished product, especially if at least 1 whole egg is used.*

■ Carefully slide the omelet onto a warm plate. Spoon half the reserved vegetable mixture over half the omelet, sprinkle with 2 tbsp (25 mL) cheese, and carefully fold in half. Repeat procedure for the second omelet.

SERVES 2

PER SERVING
*130 calories*
*4.5 g fat*
*31% calories from fat*

# Pasta and Pizza

## Forgive Me For I Have Binged

It can happen to anyone—that unguarded moment called being human. You come home tired and hungry after a long day. Before you know it, you are into an eating marathon. You feel so guilty, so desperate, that you continue eating long into the night. What hurts most is not the extra calories consumed but the way you react—overreact, as is usually the case—to your mistake.

If you do succumb, try to view the setback for what it is—temporary. Examine how you set yourself up for a binge in the first place. If you are on a restricted diet, it's easy to fall victim to overeating, or maybe your binge is a symptom of stress or anxiety. Whatever the reason, reframe your attitude about the setback. Replace your former why-bother-I've-already-blown-it mentality, which encourages you to keep overeating, with a press-on-regardless mindset. Stay calm, go for a long walk, and stay off the scale. Restrict your fat intake, and in a few days your belt will fit back into its usual notch.

If you allow yourself to be consumed by guilt, you are setting yourself up for more than the occasional binge. You are courting failure. Instead of viewing your lapse as a sign of defeat, turn it into an opportunity for self-improvement leading to long-term success.

# Linguine Pescatore

*Here's a recipe for low-fat pasta and seafood from Franko Imbrogno, owner of the Mangia Mangia Bistro Bar in Edmonton.*

| | | |
|---|---|---|
| 2 tbsp | onions, finely chopped | 25 mL |
| 1 ½ | cloves garlic, crushed | 1 ½ |
| 2 tsp | olive oil | 10 mL |
| ½ tsp | oregano | 2 mL |
| ¼ tsp | dried red chili pepper, crushed | 1 mL |
| 1 | 28 oz (796 mL) can plum tomatoes plus juice | 1 |
| ½ tsp | salt | 2 mL |
| ¼ cup | dry white wine | 50 mL |
| ¼ tsp | freshly ground pepper | 1 mL |
| 8 oz | shrimp, raw, peeled, deveined | 250 g |
| 1 lb | scallops, raw | 500 g |
| 1 lb | mussels | 500 g |
| 8 oz | squid, cooked (optional) | 250 g |
| 12 oz | linguine | 350 g |

Cut cooked squid into bite-size pieces. Set aside.

Scrub mussels and discard any that do not close when tapped. Trim any hairy beards. Bring water to a boil in a large pot. Add mussels, cover and cook over medium-high heat for 5 to 7 minutes, or until mussels open. Discard any that do not open. Drain and set aside.

Sauté onions and two-thirds of the garlic in 1 tsp (5 mL) oil until transparent. Add oregano, chili pepper, tomatoes, and salt. Bring to a boil and simmer for 30 minutes.

In a large frying pan, heat the rest of the oil gently. Add the remaining garlic and cook for 30 seconds without browning. Add white wine, pepper, shrimp, and scallops. Sauté for 1 to 2 minutes, or until scallops just turn opaque and shrimp are pink. Add cooked squid and mussels. Season with pepper. Combine with tomato sauce.

Cook linguine according to package directions. Spoon sauce over pasta and serve hot.

SERVES 6

PER SERVING
*268 calories*
*4.2 g fat*
*11 % calories from fat*

# Fettuccine with Oyster Mushrooms and Celery

*A dish perfect with grilled tuna and a glass of white wine.*

| | | |
|---|---|---|
| ¾ lb | fresh oyster mushrooms | 375 g |
| 1 tbsp | olive oil | 15 mL |
| 1 tsp | sesame oil | 5 mL |
| 2 cups | inner celery stalks, thinly sliced | 500 mL |
| 3 | cloves garlic, finely chopped (1 tbsp/15 mL) | 3 |
| ½ cup | defatted beef broth, sodium reduced | 125 mL |
| 1 tsp | grated lemon zest salt and freshly ground pepper | 5 mL |
| ½ cup | fresh parsley, finely chopped | 125 mL |
| ¾ lb | fettuccine or linguine | 375 g |
| 2 tbsp | fresh lemon juice | 25 mL |

■ Wash and cut oyster mushrooms in half.

■ Heat olive oil and sesame oil in a very large frying pan over high heat.

■ Add celery and mushrooms and toss for 1 minute. Add garlic and toss for 1 minute. Add broth, cover and cook for 1 minute, or until the mushrooms are tender but the celery is still quite crisp. If necessary, uncover and boil a moment longer to evaporate liquid. Stir in lemon zest, salt, pepper, and parsley. Toss to blend.

■ Cook pasta in boiling salted water until al dente, 2 to 5 minutes. Drain well, then combine in a heated dish with the vegetables. Season with lemon juice.

SERVES 4

PER SERVING
*240 calories*
*7 g fat*
*26% calories from fat*

# Penne Pesto

*Traditional pesto sauce is about 50 percent fat. When I am dining out I won't even consider it. I only eat pasta with pesto at home when I can use this surprisingly great-tasting recipe that doesn't taste like a compromise at all.*

| | | |
|---|---|---|
| 12 oz | penne pasta | 375 g |

**PESTO**

| | | |
|---|---|---|
| 3 tbsp | pine nuts | 45 mL |
| ½ cup | fresh basil leaves only | 125 mL |
| ½ cup | fresh spinach leaves | 125 mL |
| 2 | cloves garlic, minced | 2 |
| 2 tbsp | olive oil | 25 mL |
| ⅓ cup | defatted chicken broth | 75 mL |
| ½ cup | Parmesan cheese, grated | 125 mL |

Cook the pasta according to package directions. Drain and set aside. If necessary, cover to keep warm.

Meanwhile, preheat the oven to 400 F (200 C). Place the pine nuts on a cookie sheet. Bake for 2 to 3 minutes, or until lightly golden. Watch carefully to prevent overtoasting.

Transfer the pine nuts to a blender or food processor. Add the basil, spinach, and garlic. Process until finely chopped. With the machine running, slowly add the olive oil in a thin stream. Then slowly pour in the chicken broth and gradually add the Parmesan cheese until a paste forms.

Add the pesto to the hot pasta. Toss until well coated.

SERVES 6

---

PER SERVING
*330 calories*
*11 g fat*
*30% calories from fat*

## Know Your Olive Oil

Today, the health conscious eater's oil of choice is olive oil. It's trendy, expensive, and yes, fattening. But the good news is that olive oil is a monosaturated fat which tends to have a neutral effect on blood cholesterol levels and may lower low density lipoprotein (LDL) cholesterol.

Not all olive oils are created equal. The barometer of quality is confirmed by the price tag.

- Extra-virgin olive oil is the most expensive at eight to thirty dollars per liter. It is processed once and is very low in acidity and high in flavor. Extra-virgin olive oil is best straight out of the bottle, drizzled over salads, cooked vegetables, or bread. It's the perfect substitute for butter.

- Pure olive oil, priced at five to eight dollars per liter, is a blend of virgin and reprocessed olive oil and is recommended for cooking.

- Light olive oil has the same number of calories as other olive oils and is called light only because of its milder, olive taste and lighter color.

- Should you find olive oil at two to three dollars per liter, it's probably pomace. Producers use chemicals to extract one more grade, olive pomace oil, from the paste leftover after the first olive pressing.

*Olive oil keeps for at least a year and should be stored in an airtight container in a cool, dark place. Keep it handy and you will use it up before it has a chance to expire. Learn to replace butter and other fats with olive oil, and you will acquire one more delicious habit towards a healthier lifestyle. When it comes to flavor, a good quality olive oil goes a long way.*

# Fettuccine with Creamy Clam Sauce

*If you're looking for a cream sauce for pasta, this recipe is for you.*

| | | |
|---|---|---|
| 2 | 6 oz (184 g) cans minced clams | 2 |
| ¾ cup | defatted chicken broth | 175 mL |
| 1 cup | evaporated skim milk | 250 mL |
| 1 cup | mushrooms, sliced | 250 mL |
| ¼ cup | fresh parsley, chopped | 50 mL |
| ½ cup | green onions, chopped | 125 mL |
| 4 oz | low-fat cream cheese | 125 g |
| ¾ cup | low-fat cottage cheese | 175 mL |
| 2 tbsp | fresh lemon juice | 25 mL |
| 6 cups | fettuccine, cooked | 1.5 L |
| ⅓ cup | Parmesan cheese, grated | 75 mL |

Drain the liquid from the clams into a saucepan. Set clams aside. Add the chicken broth, milk, sliced mushrooms, parsley, and onions. Bring to a boil over medium heat and cook for approximately 10 minutes, or until liquid is reduced by half.

Cut cream cheese into cubes and add to sauce. Stir until melted.

Puree cottage cheese in blender until smooth, then add to the sauce. Stir in clams and lemon juice. Cook until hot but do not boil.

Spoon sauce over hot pasta and sprinkle with Parmesan cheese.

SERVES 6

**PER SERVING**
*322 calories*
*7 g fat*
*19% calories from fat*

# *Lasagna*

*This is a quick, fat-reduced version of an old classic.*

| | | |
|---|---|---|
| 8 oz | oven-ready lasagna noodles | 250 g |
| ½ lb | lean ground turkey | 250 g |
| 1 | 14 oz (398 mL) can stewed tomatoes, undrained | 1 |
| 1 | 14 oz (398 mL) can tomato sauce | 1 |
| ½ tsp | oregano | 2 mL |
| ½ tsp | garlic powder | 2 mL |
| ½ tsp | basil | 2 mL |
| 2 cups | low-fat ricotta cheese | 500 mL |
| ¾ cup | skim mozzarella cheese, grated | 175 mL |
| 2 tbsp | Parmesan cheese, grated | 25 mL |
| 2 tbsp | fresh parsley, chopped | 25 mL |

▤ Preheat oven to 375 F (190 C).

▤ In a nonstick frying pan, cook meat over medium heat, stirring for 3 minutes, or until no longer pink. Stir in tomatoes, tomato sauce, oregano, garlic, and basil.

▤ Spread a third of the meat sauce in the bottom of an 11 x 7-inch (28 x 18 cm) baking dish. Arrange half the uncooked noodles over the sauce. Spread half the ricotta cheese over the noodles. Top with another third of the meat sauce. Repeat, using remaining ingredients.

▤ Cover with aluminum foil and bake for 45 to 55 minutes, or until noodles are tender. Sprinkle mozzarella and Parmesan over top. Bake, uncovered, for about 5 minutes, or until cheese is melted. Let stand for 10 minutes. Sprinkle parsley over top and serve.

SERVES 6

---

PER SERVING
*380 calories*
*10 g fat*
*24% calories from fat*

## Weight Gain and Smoking

*Say it isn't so. Just as we're becoming enlightened, the Women's Movement seems to have taken two steps back for the sake of vanity. It seems some women use cigarette smoking as a means of weight control. Surveys indicate that women will soon smoke more than men. Women are more influenced by society's glamorous image of thinness than by the Surgeon General's warnings of health risks associated with smoking. They seem to be more terrified of a modest weight gain (usually about five to ten pounds) than they are of developing cancer or some other nicotine-related illness. They assume it will not happen to them. It can and it does. According to the Canadian Heart Foundation, twenty-six thousand Canadians will die of smoke-related cardiovascular ailments this year. Although the prevalence of this habit is declining, smoking is still the single most important preventable cause of death.*

*Studies indicate that smokers weigh five to ten pounds less than nonsmokers of comparable height and age. Those who quit gain about that much back, but they don't have to. Weight gain can be curtailed by eating low-fat foods and exercising.*

# Ravioli with Garlic Cream Sauce

*If you avoid cream sauces on your pasta because of the high-fat content, try this low-fat ravioli with cream sauce.*

| | | |
|---|---|---|
| 1 | head garlic | 1 |
| ¼ cup | evaporated skim milk | 50 mL |
| 1 cup | low-fat cottage cheese | 250 mL |
| 3 tbsp | fresh parsley, chopped | 45 mL |
| 2 tbsp | fresh chives, chopped | 25 mL |
| ¼ tsp | salt | 1 mL |
| ¼ tsp | freshly ground pepper | 1 mL |
| ¼ cup | Parmesan cheese, grated | 50 mL |
| 1 lb | cheese ravioli | 500 g |

▦ Preheat oven to 400 F (200 C).

▦ Remove the loose, papery skin from the garlic head without separating the cloves. Slice off ¼ inch (.5 cm) from the top of the head and discard. Wrap the garlic head in aluminum foil and roast for approximately 45 minutes, or until the garlic is very soft. Unwrap and cool enough to separate the cloves and peel.

▦ In a blender or food processor, puree garlic, milk, and cottage cheese until smooth.

▦ Cook ravioli according to package directions. While hot, toss with milk mixture, add remaining ingredients, and serve.

SERVES 4

PER SERVING
*310 calories*
*8.2 g fat*
*24% calories from fat*

# *Pizza*

The following recipe illustrates how you can substantially reduce fat in a favorite food—pizza. If you're too busy to make your own crust, you can use any ready-to-bake pizza crust. Be sure to choose a crust that hasn't been brushed with oil.

## CRUST

| | | |
|---|---|---|
| 3 ½ cups | all-purpose flour | 875 mL |
| 2 | packages instant yeast | 2 |
| 1 tsp | salt | 5 mL |
| 2 tsp | sugar | 10 mL |
| 1 tsp ea | oregano, basil, garlic power | 5 mL ea |
| 1 cup | 1% milk | 250 mL |
| 1 cup | warm water | 250 mL |

■ Coat seven 8-inch (20 cm) pizza pans with nonstick cooking spray.

■ In a large bowl, use the dough hook to combine dry ingredients. Add milk and water. Mix until dough pulls away from the sides of the bowl. Let dough rest on the table, covered, for 10 minutes. Shape dough into 7 balls. Cover and let rest for 5 minutes. Place dough in pans and push out to the edges. Keep dough covered to avoid drying out while preparing toppings.

## TOPPINGS

| | | |
|---|---|---|
| 1 ½ cups | tomato sauce | 375 mL |
| 42 | broccoli florets, blanched | 42 |
| 2 cups | mushrooms, sliced | 500 mL |
| 1 | onion, sliced | 1 |
| 8 | sun-dried tomatoes, chopped | 8 |
| 2 | small eggplants, sliced and grilled | 2 |
| | – OR – | |
| 1 | bunch or bag fresh spinach, cooked, drained and chopped | 1 |
| 1 lb | skim mozzarella cheese, grated | 500 g |

## Food Cravings

Have you ever driven miles out of your way just to satisfy some eccentric food craving? Was is for a certain brand of pizza or a particular flavor of ice cream you just couldn't live without, no matter what the cost? We don't like to admit we could go to such lengths to indulge in food cravings. It's illogical behavior for intelligent adults.

The truth is, a craving for certain foods can have physical as well as emotional reasons. Some experts suggest that cravings are biological drives to correct nutritional deficiencies, a kind of wisdom-of-the-body. We want what we need. Others suggest we crave certain foods because of the feelings they evoke.

So why do we crave certain foods and not others? Some scientists suggest cravings are a signal to eat foods that will bring about desirable mood changes. Dr. Norman Rosenthal of the National Institute of Mental Health studied people with seasonal affective disorder (SAD), also known as winter depression, and found they craved carbohydrates during the short days of fall and winter. Carbohydrates trigger a series of chemical events that stimulate the brain to produce serotonin which has a tension-relieving effect on the body. Rosenthal theorizes that we go after bread and pasta for their calming effects. Perhaps this is the *reason we refer to bread as comfort food.*

*Some animal research suggests foods with a high fat and sugar content, such as ice cream and pastries, stimulate the production of endorphins, the natural opiatelike compounds in the brain. Is it possible that a Twinkie or bowl of Haagen-Dazs at one in the morning can excite the brain's pleasure center?*

*If you are often stricken with food cravings, try to fool some of those urges with healthier alternatives. If you just can't settle for anything but the real thing, eat small portions to reduce the damage. Succumb to your cravings in moderation. Remember—"To eat is human. To fit into your clothes is divine."*

Preheat oven to 450 F (200 C).

Spread tomato sauce evenly over the pizzas. Arrange vegetables on top and sprinkle with cheese. Bake for 10 minutes, or until crust is golden brown.

SERVES 7

PER SERVING
*454 calories*
*11.9 g fat*
*23% calories from fat*

# Fish and Seafood

## Handling Seafood

Seafood is one of the healthiest foods you can eat, especially if you're trying to control your weight. Unfortunately, it does not always come from pure water. There can be a risk of contamination with eating seafood, but it's preventable. The Food and Drug Administration has the following recommendations to cut your contamination risk:

- Cook fish thoroughly. Raw seafood accounts for up to 85 percent of all seafood poisonings. Clams, mussels, and oysters should be boiled or steamed for 6 to 8 minutes (discard any unopened shells). Other fish should be cooked until it's no longer transparent and flakes easily with a fork.
- What about sushi? According to the FDA, seafood for sushi should be blastfrozen to -31 F (-35 C), or frozen at 4 F (-15 C) for seven days, to kill parasites. Your home freezer probably does not get that cold, so leave the sushi preparation to your favorite Japanese restaurant.
- Since most contaminants consolidate in fatty tissues, choose lean varieties such as snapper, cod, sole, flounder, haddock, halibut, pollock, or ocean perch. If you can, avoid fish from fresh, inland water. Choose salmon caught in the Pacific ocean or farmed in Norway or Chile.

# Salmon Cakes

*These are golden, crisp outside and creamy, rich inside. Proper eating never tasted so good.*

| | | |
|---|---|---|
| 1 lb | salmon, poached or canned, coarsely chopped | 500 g |
| ¼ cup | plain low-fat yogurt | 50 mL |
| 2 | egg whites, slightly beaten | 2 |
| ¼ cup | onion, grated | 50 mL |
| 1 tbsp | capers | 15 mL |
| 1 tbsp | fresh lemon juice | 15 mL |
| 1 tsp | fresh or dried dill | 5 mL |
| | freshly ground pepper to taste | |
| 2 cups | whole wheat breadcrumbs | 500 mL |
| 1 | lemon, cut into wedges, for garnish | 1 |
| | nonfat sour cream for garnish | |

▪ Preheat oven to 375 F (190 C).

▪ Mix all ingredients together except breadcrumbs and garnish. Mixture will be chunky. Form into 8 patties and roll patties into breadcrumbs. Place on a baking sheet sprayed with nonstick cooking spray.

▪ Bake for approximately 10 to 15 minutes, or until golden brown. Garnish with lemon wedges and nonfat sour cream if desired.

SERVES 4

PER SERVING
*213 calories*
*8 g fat*
*33% calories from fat*

# Barbecued Swordfish with Roasted Red Pepper and Ginger Sauce

*Throw some potatoes and cobs of corn on the grill, and you can prepare your entire meal outside. The colorful sauce can be served with any fish fillets.*

| | | |
|---|---|---|
| 1 | large red bell pepper | 1 |
| ¼ cup | water | 50 mL |
| ¼ tsp | white wine vinegar | 1 mL |
| | pinch salt | |
| 2 tsp | fresh ginger, grated | 10 mL |
| 4 | 4 oz (125 g) swordfish fillets | 4 |

Roast red pepper over barbecue or gas flame, turning often, until skin is blistered and blackened, or place on baking sheet in 400 F (200 C) oven for 30 minutes, turning once or twice until skin is blistered and blackened slightly. Place in plastic bag; seal and let steam 10 minutes. Scrape skin from pepper and discard seeds.

Puree pepper in a blender or food processor. Add water, vinegar, salt, and ginger and blend.

Barbecue swordfish fillets over medium coals on oiled grill, about 4 minutes on each side, or until fish is opaque. Serve each fillet with a few spoonfuls of sauce on the side.

SERVES 4

---

**PER SERVING**
*123 calories*
*1 gram fat*
*7% calories from fat*

- *Use fish within one day. When shopping, you should pick up fish as the last item on your way home. Cold rinse it, pat dry, and store in the coldest part of your refrigerator. If frozen, thaw in the refrigerator, not at room temperature.*
- *Smell it. Fish should not have a strong, fishy smell or ammonia odor. Fresh, inland fish smells like cucumbers, and ocean fish smells mildly like the ocean.*
- *The last word on fish. When in doubt, throw it out.*

# Cioppino

*The amount of olive oil in this Cioppino recipe is reduced, proving again that less is better. Serve this wonderful seafood dish with whole-grain bread and a hearty red wine. Skip the butter on your bread. Use a light sprinkling of salt instead. A crisp green salad with a low-fat salad dressing will round out this meal nicely.*

*Wine and long life? C'est impossible! When CBS's 60 Minutes publicized studies indicating that red wine may offer protection from heart attacks, North American consumption skyrocketed. The report claimed that some regions of France have lower heart disease rates despite fat consumption levels that rival those in the U.S. The so-called French Paradox Theory became a nutritional cause célèbre, greeted by wine drinkers as an affirmation of the good life.*

*Studies suggest that a daily intake of no more than 8 ounces of wine, a couple of beers or 3 ounces of 80% spirits is associated with a lower risk of heart attack. Though one French study claimed only red wine offers these benefits, other findings suggest it's the alcohol present in both red and white wines that's protective.*

*Before we enthusiastically lift up our glasses and toast to good health, we should recognize another fact. Research suggests that heavy drinking can contribute to heart disease as well as liver disease, fetal alcohol syndrome, and highway fatalities, none of which the studies considered. Remember, moderation is the key. Enjoy that glass of wine, but don't overdo it.*

| | | |
|---|---|---|
| 1 tbsp | olive oil | 15 mL |
| 1 cup | onion, diced | 250 mL |
| ½ cup | green onion, sliced | 125 mL |
| 2 | cloves garlic, crushed | 2 |
| ½ cup | dry red or white wine | 125 mL |
| ¼ cup | water | 50 mL |
| 3 tbsp | fresh parsley, chopped | 45 mL |
| 2 tsp | dried basil | 10 mL |
| ¼ tsp | dried thyme | 1 mL |
| | freshly ground pepper to taste | |
| 1 | 28 oz (796 mL) can whole tomatoes, undrained, chopped | 1 |
| 1 ½ cups | tomato puree, canned or homemade (not tomato paste) | 375 mL |
| 2 dozen | fresh mussels | 2 dozen |
| 8 oz | shrimp, raw, peeled, deveined | 250 g |
| 8 oz | fresh crabmeat | 250 g |
| 1 | 6 oz (170 mL) can minced clams, drained | 1 |
| ¼ tsp | cayenne pepper | 1 mL |

▨ In a large Dutch oven, sauté onions and garlic in oil over medium heat until tender.

▨ Add wine, water, spices, tomatoes, and tomato puree. Bring to a boil, reduce heat and simmer, covered, for 1 hour.

▨ Scrub mussels and discard any that do not close when tapped. Trim any hairy beards.

▨ Stir in mussels, shrimp, crabmeat, clams, and cayenne

pepper. Cover and simmer 20 minutes, or until seafood is done. Discard any mussels that do not open. Ladle soup into bowls and serve.

SERVES 7

PER SERVING (1 1/2 cups/375 mL)
*205 calories*
*4.2 g fat*
*18% calories from fat*

# Salmon with Dill Cream Sauce

*This elegant dish is on the Saturday evening menu at my Jasper Park Lodge Mountain Spa weekends. Although I'd rather have chef David MacGillivray and his wonderful staff prepare it, it's easy enough to make at home.*

| 4 | 5 oz (150 g) salmon fillets | 4 |
| 2 tsp | fresh lemon juice | 10 mL |
| | salt and pepper | |

Spray aluminum foil with nonstick olive oil cooking spray. Arrange salmon in a single layer. Sprinkle with lemon juice and season lightly. Fold foil over salmon and seal. Place on a baking sheet. Bake in a 400 F (200 C) oven for about 15 minutes, or until salmon is opaque and flakes easily with a fork. Serve with Dill Cream Sauce.

SERVES 4

PER SERVING (with sauce)
*280 calories*
*10.5 g fat*
*34% calories from fat*

# Dill Cream Sauce

*This multipurpose sauce works well with steamed salmon, crudities, or even as a salad dressing. If served with warm fish, the sauce should be served on the side.*

| | | |
|---|---|---|
| 2 cups | plain low-fat yogurt | 500 mL |
| 2 tsp | fresh dill, finely chopped | 10 mL |
| ½ cup | plum tomatoes, peeled, finely chopped | 125 mL |
| ¼ cup | green onions, finely chopped freshly ground pepper pinch of sugar | 50 mL |

Place yogurt in a cheesecloth-lined sieve and set over a bowl. Cover and let stand for 12 hours, or until volume of yogurt yields 1 cup (250 mL). Combine drained yogurt, dill, onions, tomatoes, and seasonings. Serve with salmon.

---

PER SERVING (1/2 cup/125 mL)
*80 calories*
*1.5 g fat*
*17% calories from fat*

## The Power of Consumers

A powerful consumer food fight has commenced lately and manufacturers are responding. Today's consumers are taking to task companies that are irresponsible and make false claims about their products. Consumers are concerned about the lack of information and misinformation about food products. They care about the use of pesticides, herbicides, and preservatives in fresh and processed foods.

Public pressure forced the ban of the cancer-causing chemical alar on apples. Red dye number two, found to induce cancer in rats, is no longer used in food products. A lone crusader in the United States led the outcry against tropical oils in cereals and cookies, and most major manufacturers responded by removing them from their products. Tuna companies changed the way they harvest tuna after children protested and boycotted their products. Progressive fast-food chains replaced Styrofoam containers with environmentally friendly packaging as a result of consumer complaints. We can make a difference and food companies are listening. They can't afford not to. Manufacturers are discovering that acting responsibly is profitable.

# Tuna and Macaroni Bake

*This casserole makes great leftovers you can munch whenever the urge strikes.*

| 2 cups | low-fat Cheddar cheese, grated | 500 mL |
| 1 | 6 oz (184 g) can tuna, packed in water, drained | 1 |
| 2 cups | macaroni, cooked | 500 mL |
| ¾ cup | evaporated skim milk | 175 mL |
| 2 tbsp | onion, finely chopped | 25 mL |
| 2 tbsp | fresh parsley, chopped | 25 mL |
| ½ tsp | salt (optional) | 2 mL |
| ¼ tsp | pepper | 1 mL |
| | paprika for topping | |

Preheat oven to 350 F (180 C).

Reserve ½ cup (125 mL) of cheese. Combine the remaining ingredients and pour into a large casserole dish coated with nonstick cooking spray. Top with reserved cheese and sprinkle with paprika. Bake for 30 minutes, or until cheese has melted.

SERVES 6

**PER SERVING**
*269 calories*
*7.8 g fat*
*26% calories from fat*

# Spanish Paella

*Since I only do easy recipes I used to be intimidated by paella, considering it too ambitious for my culinary style. In fact, it looks like more work than it actually is. The dish is named for the two-handled frying pan in which the rice is cooked and served. It is dramatic to serve and well worth the effort to make.*

| | | |
|---|---|---|
| 12 | fresh clams in shells | 12 |
| 1 lb | fresh mussels in shells | 500 g |
| 1 tbsp | olive oil | 15 mL |
| 1 lb | chicken breasts, skinless, boneless (approximately 4 half breasts) | 500 g |
| 4 | cloves garlic | 4 |
| 2 cups | uncooked rice | 500 mL |
| 3 cups | water or clam cooking liquid | 750 mL |
| 1 ½ cups | tomatoes, chopped | 375 mL |
| 1 | green bell pepper, chopped | 1 |
| 1 | bay leaf | 1 |
| 1 tsp | freshly ground pepper | 5 mL |
| | cayenne pepper to taste | |
| ¾ lb | shrimp, cleaned and cooked | 375 g |
| 1 cup | fresh or frozen peas, thawed | 250 mL |

Scrub clams and mussels under cold running water. Cut hairy beards from mussels. Discard any clams or mussels that do not close when tapped. Steam clams over boiling water until shells open, approximately 5 minutes. Reserve cooking liquid. Discard any clams that don't open. The mussels do not need to be pre-cooked. Refrigerate clams and mussels until needed.

Cut chicken into cubes. In a large, nonstick frying pan, brown chicken in oil over medium heat. Transfer chicken to paella pan or large, shallow casserole dish.

In same frying pan, cook garlic for 1 minute, then stir in rice. Add water or clam cooking liquid, tomatoes, green pepper, bay leaf, and spices. Bring to boil.

Reduce heat and simmer for 15 minutes.

■ Pour sauce over chicken. Add mussels and bake, covered, in a 425 F (220 C) oven for 20 minutes. Stir in clams, shrimp, and peas. Bake, covered, for 15 minutes, or until mussels open. Discard any mussels that don't open. Remove bay leaf before serving.

SERVES 8

PER SERVING
*280 calories*
*7 g fat*
*23% calories from fat*

# Poultry

# Lemon Chicken Stir-Fry with Glass Noodles

*Lemon and ginger scent the air as you prepare this refreshing stir-fry, which tastes as good as it smells. Don't hesitate to add your own favorite vegetables. You can't go wrong. That is the beauty of stir-frying—a most forgiving dish.*

NOTE: *Glass noodles are also called rice vermicelli and can be found in the Chinese section of the supermarket.*

| | | |
|---|---|---|
| 8 oz | chicken breast, skinless, boneless (approximately 2 half breasts) | 250 g |
| ¼ cup | water | 50 mL |
| 3 tbsp | fresh lemon juice | 45 mL |
| 2 tsp | soy sauce | 10 mL |
| 1 tsp | fresh ginger, minced – OR – | 5 mL |
| ¼ tsp | ground ginger | 1 mL |
| 1 tsp | grated lemon rind | 5 mL |
| 1 tsp | granulated sugar | 5 mL |
| 1 tsp | cornstarch | 5 mL |
| 1 tbsp | canola oil, divided | 15 mL |
| 2 | green onions, cut in 2-inch (5 cm) pieces | 2 |
| 1 | red bell pepper, cut in 1-inch (2.5 cm) pieces | 1 |
| ½ cup | snow peas | 125 mL |
| 1 cup | mushrooms, sliced | 250 mL |
| 2 oz | glass noodles | 60 g |

Cut chicken into 1-inch (2.5 cm) pieces.

In a small bowl, combine water, lemon juice, soy sauce, ginger, rind, and sugar. Mix well. Add chicken and marinate at room temperature for 30 minutes.

In a wok or small, nonstick frying pan, heat ½ tbsp (7 mL) oil over medium-high heat. Add onion, pepper, snow peas, and mushrooms and stir-fry for 2 to 3 minutes. Remove vegetables from frying pan and set aside.

▨ Add remaining oil and heat until hot. Drain chicken, reserving marinade. Add chicken to frying pan. Stir-fry until no longer pink inside.

▨ Return vegetables and marinade to frying pan for about 1 minute, or until thickened. Stir constantly.

▨ Cook noodles according to package directions. Drain. Serve chicken and vegetables over noodles.

SERVES 2

PER SERVING
*331 calories*
*8.4 g fat*
*23% calories from fat*

## The News on Cutting Boards

*Wooden cutting boards are in. Plastic boards are out. Yes, it's back to nature for chopping blocks and cutting boards. If you threw out your favorite board years ago, you are not alone. We were led to believe that the traditional wooden cutting surface as used by generations before us was a breeding ground for bacteria.*

*Research has shown that wooden cutting boards are more sanitary than plastic boards. Contaminated wooden boards stored overnight were free of bacteria the next morning, while the bacteria count soared on the plastic ones. One theory to explain the results is that wood cells absorb bacteria and entrap it permanently. The older the boards are, the better they are at canceling bacteria.*

*Regardless of what surface you use for cutting raw meat, take special care in washing the surface thoroughly with soap and hot water after each use. Plastic boards should be scrubbed well and put in the dishwasher, especially if the surface is scratched. Finally, remember to thoroughly clean your hands and any utensils you use.*

*When I inherited my mother's well-used wooden board, I replaced it with a new plastic one and it never felt quite the same. Some things, like basic kitchen tools, should never change.*

# Chicken Potpie

*The original version of chicken potpie has been nutrition-ally updated without losing any of its homespun flavor.*

### CRUST

| | | |
|---|---|---|
| 1 ½ cups | all-purpose flour | 375 mL |
| 2 tsp | baking powder | 10 mL |
| ½ tsp | salt | 2 mL |
| 3 tbsp | olive oil | 45 mL |
| ½ cup | skim milk | 125 mL |

### FILLING

| | | |
|---|---|---|
| 1 cup | defatted chicken broth | 250 mL |
| 1 cup | onion, chopped | 250 mL |
| 1 | clove garlic, crushed | 1 |
| 1 cup | mushrooms, sliced | 250 mL |
| 1 ½ lb | chicken breast, skinless, boneless (approximately 6 half breasts) | 750 g |
| 3 | medium carrots, cut into ½-inch (1 cm) slices | 3 |
| 1 cup | celery, sliced | 250 mL |
| ½ tsp | freshly ground pepper | 2 mL |
| ½ tsp ea | dried basil, thyme, tarragon | 2 mL ea |
| ½ cup | dry white wine or apple juice | 125 mL |
| 2 tbsp | cornstarch | 25 mL |
| 2 tbsp | cold water | 25 mL |

■ Preheat oven to 450 F (230 C).

■ To assemble crust, sift dry ingredients into a mixing bowl. Drizzle olive oil over mixture and stir with a fork until the texture resembles coarse cornmeal. Add milk and stir until combined. Turn dough onto a lightly floured surface and knead gently, approximately 10 times. Wrap and refrigerate.

■ Pour ¼ cup (50 mL) of the chicken broth into a frying pan and sauté onions, garlic, and mushrooms over medium heat until tender. Cut chicken into 1-inch

(2.5 cm) pieces. Add chicken, carrots, celery, and spices. Pour in wine and remaining broth. Cover and simmer for 30 minutes.

Mix cornstarch and water. Remove ¼ cup (50 mL) of the hot broth from the frying pan and stir into the cornstarch mixture. Add back into the chicken mixture, stirring constantly. Simmer and stir until smooth and thick, about 2 to 3 minutes.

Spoon filling into a medium-size casserole dish.

On a lightly floured surface, roll out dough to fit the top of the casserole. Place dough over casserole and seal against the sides of the dish with the tines of a fork. Puncture top and bake for approximately 15 minutes, or until crust is golden brown. Cover loosely with aluminum foil and bake for an additional 15 minutes, or until filling is bubbling.

SERVES 6

PER SERVING
*401 calories*
*10 g fat*
*22% calories from fat*

# Tandoori Chicken

*Tandoori chicken is a good menu choice when you are dining out. Order it skinless or remove the skin yourself when served. Rice and a green salad are perfect accompaniments to this mouth-watering chicken dish.*

| | | |
|---|---|---|
| 1 ½ lbs | chicken breasts, skinless, boneless (approximately 6 half breasts) | 750 g |
| | juice of two lemons | |
| 1 cup | plain low-fat yogurt | 250 mL |
| 2 tbsp | tamari or soy sauce 25 mL | |
| 1 tsp | ground coriander | 5 mL |
| 1 tbsp | ground cumin | 15 mL |
| 1 tbsp | turmeric | 15 mL |
| 1 tsp | fennel seeds | 5 mL |
| ½ tsp | cayenne | 2 mL |
| 3 | cloves garlic | 3 |
| 1 | large shallot, chopped | 1 |

Mix all ingredients except chicken in food processor. Place chicken in a shallow dish and pour marinade over chicken. Add enough water to cover. Marinate at least 4 hours, or overnight.

Cook chicken on a hot grill for 5 to 7 minutes, or until done. Serve hot.

SERVES 6

---

**PER SERVING**
*167 calories*
*3.1 g fat*
*17% calories from fat*

*Salad Rolls with Curried Peanut Sauce    Page 29*

*Cream of Wild Mushroom Soup    Page 39*

*Primavera Pasta Salad    Page 48*

*Spinach Phyllo Casserole    Page 59*

*Linguine Pescatore    Page 72*

*Salmon Cakes    Page 82*

*Chicken Fajitas    Page 97*

*Tea Scones*   *Page 151*

# Chicken Fajitas

*Challenge your hot–taste barometer with this hot and spicy recipe.*

| | | |
|---|---|---|
| 8 oz | chicken breasts, skinless, boneless (approximately 2 half breasts) | 250 g |
| 2 tbsp | fresh lime juice | 25 mL |
| 1 | green bell pepper, seeded and thinly sliced | 1 |
| 1 | large onion, thinly sliced | 1 |
| ½ cup | defatted chicken broth | 125 mL |
| 4 | 8-inch (20 cm) flour tortillas | |
| 3 tbsp | nonfat sour cream | 45 mL |
| 3 tbsp | plain low-fat yogurt | 45 mL |
| 1 tbsp | fresh cilantro, chopped | 15 mL |
| 1 tsp | hot pepper, finely chopped | 5 mL |
| ⅛ tsp | ground cumin | .5 mL |
| 1 cup | shredded lettuce | 250 mL |
| 1 | large ripe tomato, chopped | 1 |

■ Preheat oven to 350 F (180 C).

■ Slice chicken breasts into thin slices and sprinkle with lime juice. Marinate at room temperature for 15 minutes.

■ In a nonstick frying pan over medium heat, sauté green pepper and onions in chicken broth for approximately 1 minute. Add chicken strips and sauté until meat is cooked and liquid has evaporated.

■ To warm the tortillas, wrap in foil and place in oven for approximately 10 minutes.

■ In a small bowl, stir together sour cream, yogurt, cilantro, hot pepper, and cumin.

■ To assemble fajitas, divide chicken and vegetable mixture evenly among the tortillas. Top with sour

The hotter the better? If you love spicy food, you can rejoice at the current data on hot peppers. The chemical in peppers that gives them their fiery taste and health value is called capsaicin. Studies suggest that capsaicin has curative properties, anticancer effects, and may even influence weight loss. Dermatologists at the University of California have discovered capsaicin salve applied as an ointment stops pain and causes surgical wounds to heal faster than most ointments currently used. And researchers at Loma Linda University School of Medicine in California have discovered that capsaicin prevents the liver from turning compounds such as polyaromatic hydrocarbons, found in broiled and smoked meats, into carcinogens.

Do hot peppers have a positive effect on your waistline? Researchers in Jamaica and Great Britain suggest that capsaicin in the form of peppers causes the body to burn up to 24 percent more calories during the day than it otherwise would. Sounds interesting. Just don't forgo your morning run for a bowl of cereal laced with hot peppers.

Hot peppers are low in calories, contain just a trace of fat, and are rich in vitamins A and C. They increase salivation, improve digestion, and make even the blandest food come alive.

cream mixture and add lettuce and tomatoes. Roll up and serve immediately.

Serves 4

**PER SERVING**
*221 calories*
*5.5 g fat*
*22% calories from fat*

# Mexican Turkey Casserole

*This dish is a hearty meal minus the usual calories.*

| 1 lb | turkey breast, skinless, cooked | 500 g |

**SAUCE**

| 2 | 10 oz (284 mL) cans calorie-reduced cream of chicken soup | 2 |
| ½ cup | green onions, chopped | 125 mL |
| 1 | 12 oz (350 mL) can evaporated skim milk | 1 |
| 1 | 7 ½ oz (215 g) can green chilis, diced | 1 |
| 1 cup | low-fat Cheddar cheese, grated | 250 mL |
| 1 bag | baked tortilla chips, 8 oz (250 g) | 1 bag |

**TOPPING**

| 1 cup | low-fat Cheddar cheese, grated | 250 mL |
| 1 cup | tomatoes, diced | 250 mL |
| 1 cup | green bell pepper, diced | 250 mL |

■ Preheat oven to 350 F (180 C).

■ Shred cooked turkey and set aside.

■ In a large saucepan, combine soup, onion, milk, chilis, and cheese. Stir over medium heat until cheese is melted.

■ Spray a 13 x 19-inch (33 x 48 cm) pan with nonstick cooking spray. Line the bottom with a third of the tortilla chips. Layer a third of the turkey and a third of the sauce. Repeat twice. Sprinkle with cheese and green pepper.

■ Bake in oven for 30 to 45 minutes, or until cheese is bubbling. Sprinkle with diced tomatoes and serve hot.

SERVES 6

---

PER SERVING
*412 calories*
*6.6 g fat*
*14% calories from fat*

## Hold the Mayo?

It's summertime and the cooking should be easy. Outdoor barbecues and picnics mean countless sandwiches and millions of hot dogs and hamburgers. They would all be ho-hum without mayonnaise, ketchup, and other condiments, but those little extras aren't always as innocent as they seem. How you dress up your food can make a significant difference to how healthy it is.

Most condiments contain sugar and salt, and some have fats and preservatives as well. There is no need to be confused by condiments if you are aware of what's in them. Ketchup and dill pickles on your burger, for instance, can add up to 988 milligrams of sodium, so add condiments cautiously.

Should you hold the mayo? Go for mayonnaise with the least saturated fat and then use less than usual. Mix some low-fat yogurt with the mayo for extra mileage. The amount of mayonnaise you use is important, because even so-called low-calorie mayonnaise is relatively high in calories and fat.

One of the better condiment choices is mustard. Although prepared from mustard seeds which are high in fat, a small amount won't add many calories. One tablespoon contains no more than a gram of fat, very little of which is saturated.

Restrict your intake of pesto, olives, marinated artichoke

# Deluxe Turkey Burgers

*If you are not quite ready for veggie burgers, try using ground turkey for a lighter burger experience.*

| | | |
|---|---|---|
| 1 lb | ground turkey, skinless | 500 g |
| ½ cup | dried breadcrumbs (preferably whole-grain) | 125 mL |
| 1 | egg white | 1 |
| 1 tbsp | fresh lemon juice | 15 mL |
| 3 tbsp | onions, finely chopped | 45 mL |
| 2 tbsp | ketchup | 25 mL |
| 1 tsp | Worcestershire sauce | 5 mL |
| 1 tsp | soy sauce 5 mL | |
| ½ tsp | hot pepper sauce | 2 mL |
| ¼ tsp | salt | 1 mL |
| | freshly ground pepper to taste | |

Combine all ingredients and shape into 6 patties. Fry, broil, or grill patties until they are done, about 5 minutes each side.

Serve with lettuce, tomatoes, and onions on buns or in pita pockets. Use mustard instead of mayonnaise and save 11 grams of fat and 100 calories.

NOTE: *To freeze, place raw patties on a baking sheet and freeze until solid. Place foil or paper plates between each patty and package in freezer bags.*

SERVES 6

PER SERVING
*170 calories*
*3.6 g fat*
*19% calories from fat*

# Peach Chicken with Basmati Rice

*Did you know that cooking chicken with the skin on and removing it afterward represents the same amount of fat grams as cooking it without the skin? It you find your chicken dries out when baking, try leaving the skin on and removing it after it's cooked. Healthy cooking just keeps getting easier if you know the tricks and tips. This simple way to cook chicken is one of my favorites.*

| | | |
|---|---|---|
| 1 cup | basmati rice | 250 mL |
| 2 cups | boiling water | 500 mL |
| ½ cup | unsweetened apple juice | 125 mL |
| 2 tsp | fresh ginger, finely minced | 10 mL |
| | – OR – | |
| ½ tsp | ground ginger | 2 mL |
| ⅓ cup | fruit-sweetened apricot or peach preserves | 75 mL |
| 4 tsp | Dijon mustard | 20 mL |
| 1 lb | chicken breasts, skinless, boneless, halved (approximately 4 half breasts) | 500 g |
| 2 | peaches, sliced, canned or fresh | 2 |
| 4 | small sprigs fresh mint | 4 |

In a small saucepan, add rice to boiling water, cover and cook over low heat for 50 minutes.

Meanwhile, simmer juice and ginger in saucepan, covered, for 3 minutes. Stir in preserves and mustard. Add chicken to pan, turning to thoroughly coat. Simmer, covered, for 10 minutes, or until chicken is done.

Arrange rice and chicken on plates, top with peaches and garnish with mint.

SERVES 4

PER SERVING
*260 calories*
*3 g fat*
*10% calories from fat*

hearts, and mayonnaise-based items such as tartar sauce. Be suspicious of special or secret sauces. If I don't know what's in it, I don't want it.

Shop for condiments with short, simple ingredients that sound familiar to you. Spice up your foods in a healthier way by using salsa, pimentos, or relish. You can add flavor without compromising nutrition by choosing condiments wisely.

### Eat More and Weigh Less

*Did you know that most women experience hunger throughout the day? If you've been dieting more lately and disliking it more than ever, it may be time to try a new approach to weight control. Instead of less of everything in your life, try more. More food but the right kind, more activity, and more initiative.*

*If you eat high-fiber, nutrient-dense foods that are low in fat, you will reduce body fat and feel healthier. Instead of drinking half a cup of orange juice, eat a whole orange. The calories are the same; the only difference is fiber. Instead of potato chips, eat popcorn. I never drink apple juice; an apple takes longer to consume and is a more satisfying snack. Fiber holds food in your stomach longer, slows calorie absorption, and prevents a rapid rise in blood sugar thus staving off hunger a little longer. By eating more high-volume, low-fat foods, you can cut your calorie intake in half. Instead of worrying about eating too much, concentrate on eating well.*

# Chicken Cordon Bleu

*If you are cooking for yourself, the following recipe can be successfully frozen into individual servings.*

| | | |
|---|---|---|
| 1 ½ lb | chicken breasts, skinless, boneless (approximately 6 half breasts) | 750 g |
| 6 slices | lean ham | 6 slices |
| 6 | thin slices, skim mozzarella cheese | 6 |
| ½ cup | flour | 125 mL |
| ½ tsp | salt | 2 mL |
| 1 tsp | pepper | 5 mL |
| 3 | egg whites | 3 |
| 2 tbsp | skim milk | 25 mL |
| ¾ cup | breadcrumbs | 175 mL |
| 3 tbsp | diet margarine or butter, melted | 45 mL |

Preheat oven to 400 F (200 C).

Pound chicken breast to ¼-inch (.5 cm) thickness. Layer ham and cheese on each breast and roll up. Secure with a toothpick.

Mix flour, salt, and pepper in a shallow dish. In a separate dish beat egg whites and milk. Roll chicken bundles in flour mixture, then egg mixture, and finally coat with breadcrumbs.

Place chicken bundles, seam-side down, into a shallow baking dish coated with nonstick cooking spray. Drizzle with butter or margarine. Bake in oven for 20 to 30 minutes, or until chicken is done.

SERVES 6

PER SERVING
*351 calories*
*9.3 g fat*
*23% calories from fat.*

# Meat

# Satay Daging with Malaysian Peanut Sauce

*This version of Satay Daging is delicious! It proves once again that when it comes to eating smart, everything is possible.*

**SATAY**

| | | |
|---|---|---|
| 2 | lemon grass stalks, sliced diagonally | 2 |
| ½ | medium onion, coarsely chopped | ½ |
| 2 | large cloves garlic | 2 |
| 1 slice | fresh ginger, ¼-inch (.5 cm) thick | 1 slice |
| ¼ cup | light soy sauce | 50 mL |
| 2 tsp | turmeric | 10 mL |
| 1 tsp | sugar | 5 mL |
| ½ tsp ea | ground cumin, salt, coarse black pepper | 2 mL ea |
| 1 lb | trimmed sirloin steak | 500 g |

**MALAYSIAN PEANUT SAUCE**

| | | |
|---|---|---|
| ¼ tsp | shrimp paste 1 mL | |
| 2 | shallots, chopped | 2 |
| ¼ tsp | chili powder | 1 mL |
| 1 | large clove garlic, crushed | 1 |
| 1 | lemon grass stalk, sliced | 1 |
| ½ tsp | tamarind paste | 2 mL |
| ¼ tsp | sugar | 1 mL |
| 1 tbsp | toasted coconut | 15 mL |
| 2 tbsp | unsalted, dry-roasted peanuts, finely chopped | 25 mL |
| 8 tbsp | water | 120 mL |

▪ Place all ingredients for satay, except meat, in a blender or food processor. Process as finely as possible. Scrape mixture into a medium-size bowl.

▪ Cut meat into thin strips and cover with mixture. Marinate in refrigerator for 2 hours, or overnight.

Bring to room temperature before grilling. Skewer, using either bamboo or metal skewers. Grill over barbecue, or alternately, under oven broiler using high temperature. Cook approximately 5 minutes on each side, or to desired doneness. Serve with peanut sauce.

To prepare peanut sauce, cook shrimp paste in a small frying pan over medium heat, stirring constantly for 2 minutes, or until dry and crumbly. Set aside to cool.

In a food processor or blender, combine the shrimp paste, shallots, chili, garlic, lemon grass, and 2 tbsp (25 mL) water. Process until smooth.

In a small saucepan, bring the remaining water to boil. Add tamarind and stir to dissolve. Add the shrimp paste mixture and sugar. Simmer over low heat for 5 minutes, stirring occasionally, until slightly thickened. Stir in coconut and finely chopped peanuts. Cool.

NOTE: *If using bamboo skewers, soak them in water for at least 30 minutes before using to prevent burning.*

SERVES 10

PER SERVING
*90 calories*
*3.8 g fat*
*38% calories from fat*

# Individual Beef Wellington

*The small amount of sweet Marsala wine in this recipe goes a long way when shared with six people. This rendition is wrapped in phyllo pastry, which is lower in fat than the classic version, and topped with a mushroom mixture rather than the usual pâté de foie gras, a high fat and calorie addition. The next time you are offered pâté, keep in mind that goose liver pâté and pâté de foie gras have 60 calories and 6 grams of fat per tablespoon. Spread that cracker thinly!*

| | | |
|---|---|---|
| 1 ½ cups | fresh mushrooms, finely chopped | 375 mL |
| ¼ cup | shallots, chopped | 50 mL |
| 2 | cloves garlic, crushed | 2 |
| 2 tsp | all-purpose flour | 10 mL |
| ½ tsp | dried basil | 2 mL |
| ⅛ tsp | pepper | .5 mL |
| 2 tbsp | fresh parsley, chopped | 25 mL |
| 1 | 10 oz (284 mL) can beef consommé | 1 |
| 6 | 4 oz (125 g) beef tenderloin steak, 1-inch (2.5 cm) thick | 6 |
| 1 tbsp | Worcestershire sauce | 15 mL |
| 6 | sheets phyllo pastry | 6 |
| 1 tbsp | cornstarch | 15 mL |
| 1 ½ tsp | cornstarch | 7 mL |
| ½ cup | Marsala wine or other sweet wine | 125 mL |

▪ Preheat oven to 425 F (220 C).

▪ In a frying pan coated with nonstick cooking spray, sauté mushrooms, shallots, and garlic for approximately 2 minutes over medium heat. Stir in flour, basil, pepper, and parsley. Gradually add ¼ cup (50 mL) consommé. Stir well. Cook, stirring constantly for 5 minutes, or until liquid evaporates. Set aside.

▪ Trim fat from steaks. Coat a large frying pan with

nonstick cooking spray and place over medium-high heat until hot. Add steaks and brown 1 ½ minutes on each side. Place steaks on a broiler pan sprayed with nonstick cooking spray. Drizzle Worcestershire sauce over each steak and top with mushroom mixture.

■ Working with one phyllo sheet at a time, lightly coat the sheet with nonstick cooking spray. Fold phyllo sheet crosswise in half. Lightly coat with nonstick cooking spray and fold again to form a smaller rectangle. Spray and fold once more to form a smaller rectangle. The phyllo should be folded three times, spraying each time. Prepare remaining phyllo sheets. Drape the folded phyllo sheets over the steaks, tucking edges under. Lightly coat with nonstick cooking spray. Bake for 15 minutes, or until steaks are done to taste.

■ Stir remaining consommé, wine, and cornstarch in a small saucepan. Bring to a boil and cook for 1 minute, stirring constantly. Serve with steaks.

SERVES 6

PER SERVING
*295 calories*
*9.4 g fat*
*28% calories from fat*

*the body to burn more calories, even at rest, and regular exercise for those past sixty can raise the resting metabolism rate by as much as 10 percent.*

*The sooner you get started on your life-preserving journey the better. Proper eating and exercise should be a lifetime habit rather than a belated intervention to restore lost health.*

# Grilled Butterflied Leg of Lamb

*Butterflied legs of lamb are boned and then partially cut open so the meat can be spread apart like two butterfly wings. It's a succulent meat, perfect for special occasions.*

| | | |
|---|---|---|
| 1 | 4 to 5 lb (2 to 2.5 k) leg of lamb, butterflied and trimmed of fat | 1 |
| 3 | cloves garlic, cut into slivers | 3 |
| 1 cup | dry red wine | 250 mL |
| ½ cup | low-sodium soy sauce | 125 mL |
| 2 tbsp | rice wine vinegar | 25 mL |
| 2 tbsp | Dijon mustard | 25 mL |
| ¼ cup | fresh rosemary, chopped | 50 mL |
| | – OR – | |
| 2 tsp | dried rosemary | 10 mL |
| 1 ½ tsp | freshly ground pepper | 7 mL |

Remove all visible fat from lamb. Cut slits all over the meat and insert garlic slivers. Place the lamb in a large plastic bag and set aside.

In a bowl, combine the wine, soy sauce, vinegar, mustard, mint, rosemary, and pepper. Pour the marinade into the bag with the lamb, turning to coat the meat well. Press all the air out of the bag and seal it; place in a bowl in the refrigerator. Marinate the lamb for at least 4 hours, or overnight, turning occasionally.

Remove the lamb from the refrigerator 1 hour before grilling. Prepare a charcoal or gas grill or preheat broiler. Drain the lamb and grill for about 15 minutes on each side, basting frequently with the marinade. Let the lamb stand for about 5 minutes, then cut into thin, diagonal slices.

SERVES 12

---

**PER SERVING**
*210 calories*
*6.9 g fat*
*30% calories from fat*

# Beef Stroganoff

*The following recipe illustrates how you can very easily decrease the fat content of a traditional dish by changing a few simple ingredients.*

| | | |
|---|---|---|
| 12 oz | top round steak | 375 g |
| 2 cups | fresh mushrooms, sliced | 500 mL |
| ½ cup | onions, chopped | 125 mL |
| 1 | clove garlic, crushed | 1 |
| 3 tbsp | all-purpose flour | 45 mL |
| 1 ¼ cups | water | 300 mL |
| 1 tbsp | tomato paste | 15 mL |
| 1 tsp | instant beef bouillon powder | 5 mL |
| 1 cup | plain low-fat yogurt | 250 mL |
| 2 tbsp | dry white wine | 25 mL |
| 3 cups | cooked rice | 750 mL |

Spray a large frying pan with nonstick cooking spray. Cut meat into thin strips and brown in pan. Stir in mushrooms, onions, and garlic. Cook for 3 to 4 minutes, or until tender. Add a bit of water as necessary to avoid sticking. Remove meat and vegetables from pan and set aside.

Add 1 tbsp (15 mL) flour to frying pan. Add water, tomato paste, and bouillon. Cook and stir until thickened.

In a small bowl, mix together yogurt and 2 tbsp (25 mL) flour. Add to frying pan.

Return meat and vegetable mixture to frying pan and cook over medium heat until bubbly. Then cook and stir for 1 minute longer. Stir in wine and serve over rice.

SERVES 4

PER SERVING
*345 calories*
*7 g fat*
*18% calories from fat*

- obsessive tendencies concerning body weight such as constantly weighing yourself or overtraining;
- avoidance of social situations that involve food;
- over-restrictive or unsafe eating habits such as eliminating entire food groups;
- redness and puffiness around the eyes caused by vomiting;
- abnormal sleeping habits and hyperactivity;
- poor circulation and menstruation cessation caused by a slow metabolism, the result of starvation.

# Beef Stew

*Most of the basic food groups needed for a well-balanced diet are found in this stew.*

| | | |
|---|---|---|
| 1 ½ lb | lean beef steak, cut into 1-inch (2.5 cm) cubes | 750 g |
| 1 tbsp | canola oil | 15 mL |
| 4 | large onions, diced | 4 |
| 2 cups | mushrooms, trimmed and halved | 500 mL |
| 1 | 14 oz (398 mL) can whole tomatoes, chopped, plus juice | 1 |
| 1 | large clove garlic, crushed | 1 |
| 1 tbsp | sugar | 15 mL |
| 1 tsp | paprika 5 mL | |
| ½ tsp | freshly ground pepper | 2 mL |
| 3 tbsp | cornstarch | 45 mL |
| 1 cup | plain low-fat yogurt | 250 mL |
| 1 lb | noodles or spatzzle | 500 g |
| 2 tbsp | fresh parsley, chopped | 25 mL |

▪ In a Dutch oven, brown the beef in oil. Remove meat and set aside.

▪ Add onions to pan and sauté in oil until transparent. Add tomatoes plus juice, mushrooms, and spices and bring to a boil. Return meat to the pan and simmer, covered, over low heat for approximately 1 hour.

▪ Mix cornstarch and yogurt and add to the stew. Cook, stirring, for 1 minute.

▪ Meanwhile, boil the noodles or spatzzle. Drain. Serve the stew over the noodles and garnish with parsley.

SERVES 6

PER SERVING
*610 calories*
*11 g fat*
*16% calories from fat*

# Black Tie Burgers

*This recipe features an upscale version of the humble hamburger. I once had this burger at a trendy Toronto restaurant many years ago. As well as being fattening, the price of the entrée was as fancy as the restaurant that served it. This version is easy on your budget as well as your waistline.*

### PATTIES

| | | |
|---|---|---|
| 12 oz | extra-lean ground beef | 375 g |
| 2 | egg whites | 2 |
| ¼ cup | tomato puree | 50 mL |
| ½ | small green bell pepper, finely chopped | ½ |
| 1 | green onion, finely chopped | 1 |
| 1 tsp | cornstarch | 5 mL |
| 1 tsp | cumin | 5 mL |
| 1 tsp | fennel seed | 5 mL |
| ½ tsp | dried red chili pepper flakes | 2 mL |
| ½ tsp | oregano | 2 mL |

### SAUCE

| | | |
|---|---|---|
| ½ tsp | garlic powder | 2 mL |
| 1 | medium tomato, finely chopped | 1 |
| 1 cup | tomato sauce | 250 mL |
| ¼ tsp | oregano | 1 mL |

### TOPPING

| | | |
|---|---|---|
| 2 oz | skim mozzarella cheese (4 thin slices) | 50 g |
| 2 tbsp | light Parmesan cheese, grated | 25 mL |
| 4 | slices French bread, 1-inch (2.5 cm) thick | 4 |

▢ Preheat oven to 450 F (230 C).

▢ Combine all ingredients for patties and mix well. Shape into 4 patties, about ¾-inch (2 cm) thick. Bake for 5 minutes. Turn and bake for 3 more minutes, or until done.

### Hamburger Disease

The rare hamburger should be a thing of the past. How do you like your burger? There is only one way to answer that popular, barbecue-season question. Better say "Well done!" Public health officials regularly ask the media to alert people to the dangers of Hamburger Disease or Barbecue Syndrome. E-coli, the culprit, is a common bacterium normally found in the intestines and feces of humans and other animals. If ingested, however, E-coli can cause bloody diarrhea, stomach cramps, and vomiting as well as the more grave hemolytic uremic syndrome (HUS), which affects the kidneys and blood. The illness usually involves hospitalization and lasts seven to ten days. Most people recover without complications, although HUS can be fatal, especially for children.

Protection against the disease is simple. Cook ground meats to 155 F (74 C) until well done. The center should look gray. Smelling the meat will not help determine its condition since meat contaminated with E-coli does not have an odor. Steaks, chops, and other whole meats pose much less risk than ground meats which offer microorganisms more surfaces on which to multiply. When it comes to ground meats, play it safe. Just say "No" to rare.

■ Meanwhile, combine all ingredients for sauce and simmer at low temperature for 5 minutes, or until thickened. Place each patty on toasted bread and top with sauce. Arrange mozzarella slices over sauce and sprinkle with Parmesan cheese. Return to oven and bake until cheese is melted and meat is thoroughly cooked.

SERVES 4

PER SERVING
325 calories
10 g fat
27% calories from fat

# Roasted Vegetables and Lamb Muffaletta

*The muffaletta sandwich is a flavorful combination of lamb and vegetables. Give this one a try.*

| | | |
|---|---|---|
| 2 | grilled lamb chops, fat removed | 2 |
| 1 | medium eggplant | 1 |
| ½ tbsp | olive oil | 7 mL |
| 1 | jar roasted red peppers, packed in water, drained and chopped | 1 |
| 4 oz | feta cheese | 125 g |
| 1 tsp | fresh lemon juice | 5 mL |
| 2 tsp | fat-free Italian dressing | 10 mL |
| | salt and freshly ground pepper | |
| 1 | round loaf bread, about 9 inches (23 cm) across | 1 |

Remove fat from lamb chops. Grill and sliver. Set aside.

Cut eggplant into ½-inch (1 cm) slices. Brush both sides with olive oil. Broil or grill 3 to 4 minutes on each side, or until browned.

Chop cooked eggplant and mix with lamb chops and red peppers.

In a small bowl, mash feta cheese with a fork. Mix with lemon juice and Italian dressing.

Slice bread in half horizontally. Scoop out 1 inch (2.5 cm) of the soft interior from each half. Spread the feta mixture evenly on the bottom half of the loaf. Spoon the eggplant mixture over the feta and top with other half of bread. Cut into 6 wedges. Serve warm or cold.

SERVES 4

PER SERVING
*346 calories*
*11.8 g fat*
*31% calories from fat*

# Desserts

# Dessert Cream Sauce

*This is great as a dip for fruit, on pancakes with fresh-cut fruit, or as a topping for desserts like baked apples.*

| 1 cup | plain low-fat yogurt | 250 mL |
| 1 tbsp | honey | 15 mL |
| 1 tsp | cinnamon | 5 mL |

▪ Combine all ingredients in a small bowl and mix together.

SERVES 4

PER SERVING (1/4 cup/50 mL)
*52 calories*
*0.7 g fat*
*13% calories from fat*

## Fresh Fruit Syrup

*Try this sauce as a topping for pancakes or crepes, cakes or biscuits.*

| | | |
|---|---|---|
| 1 cup | fresh berries | 250 mL |
| 1 tbsp | maple syrup | 15 mL |
| ¼ cup | water | 50 mL |

■ Puree all ingredients together in a blender.

SERVES 4

PER SERVING (1/4 cup/50 mL)
*30 calories*
*trace of fat*

# Peach-Raspberry Crisp

*This is my favorite way to enjoy ripe peaches when they are in abundance and I've eaten enough fresh ones.*

## FILLING

| | | |
|---|---|---|
| 6 | peaches | 6 |
| 1 ½ cups | raspberries | 375 mL |
| ¼ cup | maple syrup | 50 mL |
| 3 tbsp | brown sugar | 45 mL |
| 2 tbsp | fresh lemon juice | 25 mL |
| 2 tbsp | cornstarch | 25 mL |
| ¼ tsp | cinnamon | 1 mL |
| ¼ tsp | nutmeg | 1 mL |

## TOPPING

| | | |
|---|---|---|
| ¾ cup | packed brown sugar | 175 mL |
| ¾ cup | rolled oats | 175 mL |
| ¾ cup | all-purpose flour | 175 mL |
| 2 tsp | butter | 10 mL |
| 2 tbsp | canola oil | 25 mL |
| 2 tbsp | apple juice | 25 mL |

Preheat oven to 400 F (200 C).

Dip peaches in boiling water for approximately 20 seconds. Remove using a slotted spoon and rinse under cold water. Peel and pit peaches. Cut peaches into wedges and place in a large bowl.

Add raspberries, maple syrup, brown sugar, lemon juice, cornstarch, and spices. Place fruit mixture in a shallow baking dish.

Combine brown sugar, rolled oats, and flour in a large bowl. With two sharp knives or pastry cutter, cut in butter until crumbly. Blend in oil. Pour in apple juice and stir with a fork until blended. Distribute topping evenly over fruit.

**Desserts**

Yes, it's true. Desserts are back on the menu. We're finally becoming more relaxed about what we eat, including desserts. There is no reason to stop eating desserts; just eat less of them. If you want to lose weight, avoid the standard serving size of desserts. When dining out, order one piece with enough forks for everyone at your table. Apple pie and chocolate cake, for example, cost less than 100 calories when split three ways. A hundred calories, in fact, can mean anything from a couple of Oreos to a skinny piece of pie or a few spoonfuls of chocolate mousse. A small serving of dessert won't do much harm, yet is substantial enough to satisfy a sweet craving at the end of a meal.

Desserts do not have to be rich. The fat calories in most recipes can be slashed by one-half or more without spoiling the taste. Low-fat cheesecakes, cream sauces made with skim milk, and cakes without oil are all delicious dessert options.

■ Bake in oven for about 40 minutes, or until golden. Serve warm with low-fat ice cream or frozen yogurt.

SERVES 8

---

PER SERVING
*304 calories*
*7 g fat*
*21% calories from fat*

---

# Lemon Soufflé

*If you are looking for an elegant dessert for that special occasion, this refreshing soufflé is it.*

| ½ cup | sugar | 125 mL |
|---|---|---|
| 2 tbsp | cornstarch | 25 mL |
| 2 tsp | lemon zest, grated | 10 mL |
| ⅓ cup | fresh lemon juice | 75 mL |
| 2 tbsp | fresh orange juice | 25 mL |
| 2 tbsp | orange liqueur (such as Grand Marnier or Cointreau) | 25 mL |
| 5 | large egg whites (room temperature) | 5 |
| ¼ tsp | cream of tartar | 1 mL |
| | pinch of salt | |
| | confectioner's sugar for dusting | |

▨ Preheat oven to 350 F (180 C). Place rack in lower third of stove. Lightly coat the inside of a soufflé dish, or six ½ cup (125 mL) individual soufflé dishes, with nonstick cooking spray. Sprinkle with sugar and tap out excess.

▨ In a small, heavy saucepan, whisk together cornstarch, lemon zest, lemon juice, orange juice, and half the sugar. Bring to boil over medium heat, stirring constantly. Cook, stirring, for 30 to 45 seconds, or until slightly thickened and no longer cloudy. Remove from the heat, stir in orange liqueur and let cool to room temperature.

▨ The recipe can be prepared ahead to this point. Store, covered, in the refrigerator for up to two days. Bring to room temperature before proceeding.

▨ In a large, grease-free mixing bowl, beat egg whites with an electric mixer on medium speed until foamy and opaque. Add cream of tartar and salt. Gradually increase speed to high and beat until soft peaks form.

## Vitamins—Are You Getting Enough?

The prevalent nutritional message today is still to eat a well-balanced diet. But in order to achieve an optimal state of health, do you also have to consume supplemental levels of various vitamins and minerals?

To critics of the multimillion dollar vitamin industry, taking vitamin supplements just creates expensive urine; however, evidence trickling out of laboratories around the world suggests it's time to reconsider the role of vitamins.

According to Jeffrey Blumberg, Associate Director of the Human Nutrition Research Center on Aging at Tufts University, "I think we have enough data in hand for physicians to begin suggesting their patients take supplements, or at least not discourage them from it." Such advice must come with a warning that vitamins don't work magic. "Vitamins are like seat belts," says Dr. Blumberg. "Wearing a seat belt doesn't give you a license to drive recklessly, it just protects you in case of an accident." Vitamin supplements work the same way. They don't give you a license to eat poorly. What they do, is provide an added cushion of protection.

Slowly add the remaining sugar and beat until stiff, but not dry, peaks form.

▢ Stir the lemon mixture. Whisk about one quarter of the beaten egg whites into the lemon mixture until smooth. Using a rubber spatula, fold the lemon mixture back into the remaining whites.

▢ Turn mixture into the prepared dishes and place dishes in a roasting pan. Fill the pan with hot water about one-third up the sides of the dishes. Bake until puffed and the top feels firm to the touch, about 25 minutes for individual soufflés and about 35 minutes for a large soufflé. Dust with confectioner's sugar and serve immediately.

SERVES 6

PER SERVING
*130 calories*
*0 g fat*

# *Strawberry Brulee*

*The following dessert is an excellent way to utilize fresh fruit to increase vitamin and fiber intake.*

| 3 cups | strawberries, sliced | 750 mL |
|--------|---------------------|--------|
| 2 tbsp | sugar | 25 mL |
| 2 tsp | cornstarch | 10 mL |
| 1 | egg, lightly beaten | 1 |
| 1 cup | skim milk | 250 mL |
| 2 tbsp | nonfat sour cream | 25 mL |
| ½ tsp | vanilla extract | 2 mL |
| 2 tbsp | brown sugar | 25 mL |
| 1 tbsp | roasted almonds, sliced | 15 mL |

Place strawberries in a 9-inch (23 cm) casserole dish and set aside.

Combine sugar and cornstarch in a small saucepan and stir well. While stirring, add egg and milk gradually. Cook over low heat for 10 minutes, or until thickened, stirring constantly. Remove from heat and let cool for 5 minutes. Add vanilla and sour cream. Stir well.

Spoon custard mixture evenly over strawberries. Sprinkle with brown sugar and broil for 2 minutes, or until sugar melts. Sprinkle with almonds. Serve warm.

SERVES 4

PER SERVING
*135 calories*
*3.5 g fat*
*24% calories from fat*

# Cheese Blintzes

*This decadent dessert uses only 6.8 grams of your fat budget.*

**BATTER**

| | | |
|---|---|---|
| ¾ cup | all-purpose flour | 175 mL |
| 1 cup | skim milk | 250 mL |
| 2 | large egg whites | 2 |
| 1 | egg | 1 |
| ¼ tsp | salt | 1 mL |

**FILLING**

| | | |
|---|---|---|
| 2 cups | low-fat cottage cheese | 500 mL |
| 2 tbsp | low-fat cream cheese | 25 mL |
| 1 | large egg white | 1 |
| 2 tbsp | sugar | 25 mL |
| 1 tsp | grated lemon zest | 5 mL |
| ½ tsp | pure vanilla extract | 2 mL |

**TOPPING**

| | | |
|---|---|---|
| ½ cup | nonfat sour cream | 125 mL |
| ¼ cup | plain low-fat yogurt | 50 mL |
| 1 cup | fresh or frozen berries | 250 mL |
| 1 cup | fresh or frozen strawberries | 250 mL |
| 1 tbsp | sugar or sugar substitute | 15 mL |

▪ Preheat oven to 400 F (200 C).

▪ In a blender or food processor, combine flour, milk, egg whites, egg, and salt. Process until smooth.

▪ Spray an 8-inch (20 cm) frying pan with nonstick cooking spray and heat over medium heat. Pour in 2 tbsp (25 mL) of batter, tilting pan slowly to cover the bottom with a thin layer. Cook until the underside is golden, about 15 seconds. Slip the crepe onto a plate and repeat with remaining batter.

▪ Place cottage cheese in sieve to drain, then combine with rest of filling ingredients in a food processor and process.

■ To assemble, place 2 tbsp (25 mL) filling in the center of each crepe. Fold sides over filling and roll crepes lengthwise. Place blintzes, seam-side down, in baking dish coated lightly with nonstick cooking spray. Bake for 10 to 20 minutes, or until heated through.

■ Combine yogurt and sour cream and spoon evenly on blintzes. Mix fruit and sugar together and spread on top of each blintz. Serve hot.

SERVES 4

PER SERVING
*312 calories*
*5.8 g fat*
*17% calories from fat*

# Cakes, Pies and Tarts

# Chocolate Cheesecake

*The strategic balance of flavorings and reduction of fats achieves a cake so rich and sinful, it could fool even the most passionate chocoholic.*

CRUST

| 18 | chocolate wafers | 18 |
|---|---|---|
| 1 cup | Grapenuts cereal | 250 mL |
| 2 tbsp | sugar | 25 mL |
| 1 tbsp | unsweetened cocoa powder | 15 mL |
| 3 tbsp | canola oil | 45 mL |
| 3 tbsp | water | 45 mL |

FILLING

| 2 oz | semisweet chocolate | 50 g |
|---|---|---|
| 1 tbsp | instant coffee powder | 15 mL |
| 1 tbsp | boiling water | 15 mL |
| 4 cups | low-fat cottage cheese | 1 L |
| 1 | 8 oz (250 g) package low-fat cream cheese (room temperature) | 1 |
| 1 ½ cups | sugar | 375 mL |
| 3 | egg whites | 3 |
| 1 | egg | 1 |
| 1 cup | low-fat sour cream | 250 mL |
| 2 tbsp | cornstarch | 25 mL |
| ¾ cup | unsweetened cocoa powder | 175 mL |
| 1 tsp | vanilla | 5 mL |
| | dash salt | |

Preheat oven to 325 F (160 C). Coat a 9-inch (23 cm) springform pan with nonstick cooking spray.

To prepare crust, place wafers, cereal, sugar, and cocoa in food processor to create crumbs. Add oil and water and process until crumbs are moistened. Press crumbs into bottom and halfway up the sides of prepared pan. Set aside.

To prepare the filling, melt chocolate. Dissolve coffee in water and add to chocolate. Place cottage cheese in

### The Weight Game—Why Men Lose and Women Don't

*Men and women are not created equal, at least not when it comes to weight. Even Gloria Steinem can't rectify the unfair advantage men have over women when it comes to shedding pounds.*

*"Female fat cells are physiologically different from male fat cells," says Debra Waterhouse, a registered dietitian and author from California. "They love to store fat, but hate to give it up." Waterhouse came to that conclusion during a long career of nutritional counseling. In her book* Outsmarting the Female Fat Cell, *she explains the reason women protect their fat—the female hormone estrogen. The enzymes that store fat are called lipogenic enzymes. Estrogen activates and multiplies these enzymes, making it more difficult for women to lose weight.*

*To overcome this handicap and outsmart your fat cells, Waterhouse's advice includes regular exercise, a fat intake of 20 percent, eating often, and never overeating. By gradually making changes in your activity level and eating routine, you can successfully shed weight and keep it off.*

a piece of cheesecloth, gather into a ball, and squeeze out moisture. Put cottage cheese solids in a food processor and blend until smooth. Add the rest of the ingredients and process until smooth.

■ Pour into prepared pan and bake for about 1 hour, or until firm. The center should be slightly soft and shiny. Run a knife around the pan to loosen the edges. Cool. Cover and refrigerate at least 8 hours before serving.

SERVES 12

---

**PER SERVING**
*355 calories*
*12 g fat*
*30% calories from fat*

---

# Apple Cheesecake

*Keep the flavor of the original while chiseling away the fat.*

| | | |
|---|---|---|
| 2 cups | apple, peeled and thinly sliced | 500 mL |
| ½ tsp | cinnamon | 2 mL |
| 2 tbsp | sugar | 25 mL |
| 1 | egg | 1 |
| 2 | egg whites | 2 |
| ⅔ cup | sugar | 150 mL |
| 1 | 8 oz (250 g) package low-fat cream cheese | 1 |
| 2 ½ cups | low-fat ricotta cheese | 625 mL |
| ½ cup | buttermilk | 125 mL |
| 2 tsp | vanilla extract | 10 mL |
| 4 tbsp | all-purpose flour | 60 mL |

▩ Preheat oven to 325 F (160 C). Coat the bottom of a 9-inch (23 cm) springform pan with nonstick cooking spray. Wrap a sheet of aluminum foil around the outside of pan.

▩ Arrange sliced apples in bottom of pan. Mix cinnamon and 2 tbsp (25 mL) sugar together and sprinkle over apples.

▩ Slightly beat eggs and combine with ⅔ cup (150 mL) sugar, cheeses, buttermilk, vanilla, and flour. Beat with electric mixer until well blended. Pour cheese mixture over apples.

▩ Place pan into a large, shallow pan and add hot water to a depth of 1 inch (2.5 cm). Bake for approximately 70 minutes, or until set. Cool. Cover and refrigerate for at least 4 hours before serving.

SERVES 10

PER SERVING
*209 calories*
*4.7 g fat*
*20% calories from fat*

# Carrot Cake

*This recipe is a good example of how a dessert can be modified and still taste great.*

### CAKE

| | | |
|---|---|---|
| 1 ¼ cups | sugar | 300 mL |
| ¼ cup | canola oil | 50 mL |
| ½ cup | skim milk | 125 mL |
| ¾ cup | applesauce | 175 mL |
| 6 | egg whites | 6 |
| 2 cups | flour | 500 mL |
| 2 tsp | baking soda | 10 mL |
| 2 tsp | cinnamon | 10 mL |
| ½ tsp | nutmeg | 2 mL |
| ¼ tsp | ground cloves | 1 mL |
| 1 ½ tsp | vanilla | 7 mL |
| 2 cups | carrots, grated | 500 mL |
| ½ cup | raisins | 125 mL |
| 1 | 8 oz (250 mL) can crushed pineapple, naturally sweetened with juice | 1 |

### FROSTING

| | | |
|---|---|---|
| 1 cup | low-fat ricotta cheese | 250 mL |
| 1 | 8 oz (250 g) package low-fat cream cheese, softened | 1 |
| 2 tsp | vanilla | 10 mL |
| 1 cup | icing sugar | 250 mL |

■ Preheat oven to 350 F (180 C). Spray a 9-inch (23 cm) tube pan with nonstick cooking spray.

■ In a bowl, beat together sugar, oil, milk, applesauce, and egg whites. In another bowl, sift together flour, baking soda, cinnamon, nutmeg, and cloves. Combine ingredients from both bowls. Add vanilla, carrots, raisins, and crushed pineapple with juice. Mix well.

■ Pour batter into prepared pan. Bake for approximately 1 hour, or until toothpick inserted into thickest part of cake comes out clean. Cool for 5 minutes. Run a knife around the edges of the pan to loosen and turn the cake out onto a rack to cool.

To prepare frosting, blend cheeses and vanilla in food processor until fluffy. Add icing sugar and process until smooth. Frost cake. Add a few drops of skim milk or water if too thick to spread.

SERVES 16

PER SERVING
*287 calories*
*7.2 g fat*
*22% calories from fat*

# Chocolate Cake

*For centuries, lovers have used chocolate to say "I love you." Scientists have discovered that an ingredient in chocolate called phenlethylamine can incite passion. It is a substance nearly identical to certain hormones produced by the body during lovemaking. Casanova claimed he used chocolate instead of champagne to induce romance. Madam du Barry (Louis XV's mistress) is said to have given it to her partners as an aphrodisiac. This cupid-approved recipe yields 10 generous servings of chocolate cake. Bake at your own risk.*

### CAKE

| | | |
|---|---|---|
| 1 ¾ cups | all-purpose flour | 425 mL |
| 1 ½ cups | sugar | 375 mL |
| 1 ½ tsp | baking powder | 7 mL |
| ¾ cup | cocoa powder | 175 mL |
| 4 | egg whites | 4 |
| 1 cup | skim milk | 250 mL |
| ½ cup | unsweetened applesauce | 125 mL |
| 2 tsp | vanilla extract | 10 mL |
| 1 cup | boiling water | 250 mL |

### FROSTING

| | | |
|---|---|---|
| ¼ cup | diet margarine, room temperature | 50 mL |
| 2 tbsp | plain low-fat yogurt | 25 mL |
| 3 tbsp | skim milk | 45 mL |
| 2 tsp | vanilla extract | 10 mL |
| ½ cup | cocoa powder | 125 mL |
| 2 cups | icing sugar | 500 mL |

■ Preheat oven to 350 F (180 C). Spray two 9-inch (23 cm) cake pans with nonstick cooking spray. Lightly flour.

■ To prepare cake, combine dry ingredients. Add remaining ingredients, except water, and mix on medium speed for 2 minutes. Stir in boiling water.

■ Pour batter into prepared cake pans and bake in

oven for 25 to 30 minutes, or until center springs back when touched. Cool for 10 minutes before removing from pans. Cool cakes completely before frosting.

Prepare frosting by creaming together margarine and yogurt until smooth. In a separate bowl combine milk and vanilla. In another bowl combine coca and sugar.

Alternating milk and cocoa mixtures, add to margarine mixture until desired consistency. Add more milk if necessary.

SERVES 10

PER SERVING
*373 calories*
*4.1 g fat*
*9% calories from fat*

Exercise—Walking

Mankind's original way of getting around is also the most effective way to lose weight. Walking is the best exercise of all—a natural activity. If you don't like to exert yourself while exercising, this may be the workout for you. It's a gentle, injury-free way of getting into shape. The good news is, you can burn the same number of calories walking or running the same distance.

The equipment you need is minimal: comfortable clothing and a good pair of shoes. Let comfort and the weather be your guide. Dress in layers and try to stay cool during your walk. If you dress too warmly, you will not work as hard and, as a result, will reduce the cardiovascular benefits of your walk.

A few simple changes can help you incorporate walking into your daily routine. Instead of talking on the phone or over a cup of coffee, meet friends for a walk and get into shape while socializing. Make it a regular rendezvous, perhaps two or three times a week. If it's feasible, walk to work, the store, or to your local restaurant and burn off some calories before you arrive. So whether you stride, strut, stroll or just saunter, develop your own style and walk the road to fitness.

# Berry Coffee Cake

*Few aromas are more pleasing and spirit-lifting than the fragrance of a freshly baked coffee cake, and few make for greater nostalgia for hearth and home. This coffee cake should be eaten as freshly baked as possible. With this sumptuous recipe and a house filled with kids, leftovers won't be a problem.*

### CAKE

| | | |
|---|---|---|
| 3 tbsp | vegetable oil | 45 mL |
| 2 | egg whites | 2 |
| ½ cup | plain low-fat yogurt | 125 mL |
| ½ cup | skim milk | 125 mL |
| 1 tsp | vanilla extract | 5 mL |
| 2 cups | all-purpose flour | 500 mL |
| ½ cup | sugar | 125 mL |
| 4 tsp | baking powder | 20 mL |
| ½ tsp | salt | 2 mL |
| 1 cup | fresh or frozen blueberries | 250 mL |
| ½ cup | fresh or frozen raspberries | 125 mL |

### TOPPING

| | | |
|---|---|---|
| 2 tbsp | brown sugar | 25 mL |
| ¼ tsp | cinnamon | 1 mL |

Preheat oven to 400 F (200 C). Coat an 8-inch (20 cm) round baking pan with nonstick cooking spray

Whisk together oil, egg whites, yogurt, milk, and vanilla.

In another bowl, sift together flour, sugar, baking powder, and salt. Add to yogurt mixture along with berries and stir just to blend. Turn batter into the prepared pan.

In a small bowl, stir together sugar and cinnamon. Sprinkle over the batter.

Bake in oven for 35 to 40 minutes, or until top is

golden brown and a cake tester inserted into the middle comes out clean.

SERVES 9

PER SERVING
*231 calories*
*5.6 g fat*
*21% calories from fat*

# *Peach Almond Shortcake*

*With this shortcake recipe you can have your cake and eat it too!*

### SHORTCAKE

| | | |
|---|---|---|
| 2 ¼ cups | all-purpose flour | 550 mL |
| ⅓ cup | sugar | 75 mL |
| 1 ½ tsp | baking powder | 7 mL |
| ¾ tsp | baking soda | 4 mL |
| ¼ tsp | salt | 1 mL |
| 1 cup | buttermilk | 250 mL |
| 2 tbsp | unsalted butter | 25 mL |
| 1 tbsp | vegetable oil | 15 mL |
| ½ tsp | almond extract | 2 mL |
| ¼ cup | almonds, sliced | 50 mL |
| 1 tbsp | sugar (for tops of biscuits) | 15 mL |

### FILLING

| | | |
|---|---|---|
| 6 | ripe peaches, peeled and sliced | 6 |
| ⅓ cup | sugar | 75 mL |
| 2 cups | low-fat frozen yogurt, vanilla flavored | 500 mL |

■ Preheat oven to 425 F (220 C).

■ In a large bowl, stir together flour, sugar, baking powder, baking soda, and salt. Using a pastry blender or two knives, cut butter into mixture until crumbly.

■ In a small bowl, combine buttermilk, butter, oil, and almond extract. Make a well in the center of the dry mixture and add the buttermilk mixture. Using a fork, stir just until combined.

■ Drop by spoonfuls onto a baking sheet sprayed with nonstick cooking spray. You should have 6 biscuits. Scatter almonds over tops and sprinkle with remaining sugar. Bake in oven for approximately 15 minutes, or until golden brown.

To prepare the filling, toss sugar with peaches and let stand at least 1 hour, or until a light syrup is formed.

Using a serrated knife, split the slightly cooled biscuits. For each biscuit, set bottom part on dessert plate, spoon on peaches and syrup. Top with frozen yogurt and crown with top of biscuit. Dust with sugar. Serve immediately.

SERVES 6

PER SERVING
*420 calories*
*9.5 g fat*
*20% calories from fat*

# Pumpkin Pie

*Pumpkin pie is the perfect ending to any meal. Do your family and friends a favor by serving this lighter version of a traditional favorite.*

### CRUST

| | | |
|---|---|---|
| 1 cup | all-purpose flour | 250 mL |
| ¼ tsp | salt | 1 mL |
| ¼ cup | shortening | 50 mL |
| 2 to 3 tbsp | cold water | 30 to 45 mL |

### FILLING

| | | |
|---|---|---|
| 1 ½ cups | canned pumpkin | 375 mL |
| ¼ cup | granulated sugar | 50 mL |
| ¼ cup | maple syrup | 50 mL |
| ¾ tsp | cinnamon | 4 mL |
| ¼ tsp | ground ginger | 1 mL |
| ¼ tsp | nutmeg or mace | 1 mL |
| ¼ tsp | salt | 1 mL |
| ¾ cup | evaporated skim milk | 175 mL |
| 2 | egg yolks | 2 |
| 4 | egg whites | 4 |

Preheat oven to 400 F (200 C).

To prepare crust, blend together flour and salt. Using a pastry blender or two knives, cut in the shortening until the mixture is uniformly crumbly.

Add the water, 1 tbsp (15 mL) at a time, mixing lightly with a fork until the flour is evenly moistened. Add just enough water to permit the dough to be formed into a ball.

Turn the dough onto a piece of wax paper and form into a ball. Chill if desired. When ready to use, roll dough out on a floured surface, rolling evenly into a circle, preferable between two sheets of floured wax paper. Fit the dough into a 9-inch (23 cm) pie plate.

▧ In a large bowl, combine all ingredients for the filling, except egg whites. Beat together well. In a separate bowl, beat the egg whites until stiff. Gently fold egg whites into pumpkin mixture and blend thoroughly. Pour into prepared pie shell.

▧ Bake in oven for 10 minutes. Lower temperature to 350 F (180 C) and continue to bake for another 30 to 40 minutes, or until a tester inserted into the center of the pie comes out clean.

SERVES 6

PER SERVING
*294 calories*
*12 g fat*
*36% calories from fat*

## Weight and Gender Differences

Being female is a disadvantage when it comes to losing weight. Put men and women of equal size on restricted diets and men will lose more weight than women.

Your ability to burn calories depends primarily on your body composition. The more muscle or lean body mass you have, the faster your metabolic rate. Women, by design, have proportionately less muscle and more body fat than men.

One way to combat this is through weight training. If you've never lifted weights before, now is the time to begin. In fact, the American College of Sports Medicine has revised its position on the type of exercise necessary for adults to lead healthy lives. In the past they emphasized aerobic exercise such as running, cycling, swimming, hiking, or aerobic dancing three times a week. Now they recommend that adults include strength training in their weekly workout schedule. Research has shown that consistent strength training helps maintain muscle and bone mass, and may reduce the risk of osteoporosis and protect against postmenopausal bone loss.

So, ladies, pump up. The evidence is in. Since muscle tissue requires more caloric energy than fat tissue, your body will consume extra calories if it becomes more muscular.

# Blueberry Dream Pie

*Save room for dessert if this delicious pie is on the menu.*

### CRUST
| | | |
|---|---|---|
| 3 tbsp | melted butter | 45 mL |
| 1 cup | graham cracker crumbs | 250 mL |

### FILLING
| | | |
|---|---|---|
| 2 | ½ oz (15 g) packages unflavored gelatin powder | 2 |
| ⅔ cup | granulated sugar | 150 mL |
| 1 cup | hot water | 250 mL |
| 2 cups | low-fat blueberry yogurt | 500 mL |
| 1 cup | nonfat sour cream | 250 mL |
| 1 | envelope dessert topping mix | 1 |
| ½ cup | skim milk | 125 mL |
| 1 tsp | vanilla | 5 mL |
| 2 cups | fresh or frozen blueberries | 500 mL |

◾ Preheat oven to 350 F (180 C).

◾ Stir crust ingredients together. Press into 9 x 13-inch (23 x 33 cm) pan sprayed with nonstick cooking spray. Bake in oven for 10 minutes. Cool.

◾ Mix sugar and gelatin in saucepan and add water. Heat and stir over medium heat until dissolved. Chill until syrupy.

◾ Fold yogurt and sour cream into gelatin mixture. In a separate bowl, beat dessert topping mix, milk, and vanilla until stiff. Add to gelatin mixture and stir until blended. Fold in blueberries. If using frozen blueberries, thaw and drain well on paper towels before using. Pour mixture into prepared pan. Chill until firm.

SERVES 16

**PER SERVING**
*156 calories*
*5.2 g fat*
*30% calories from fat*

# Tropical Fruit Tart

*The following recipe proves that traditionally fattening food can still be enjoyed the low-fat way. Remember to cut portions slightly. A small treat is still a treat.*

## CRUST

| | | |
|---|---|---|
| 1 cup | pastry flour | 250 mL |
| 3 tbsp | sugar | 45 mL |
| 1 tsp | lemon peel, grated | 5 mL |
| 4 tbsp | buttermilk | 60 mL |
| 2 tbsp | canola oil | 25 mL |

## TOPPING

| | | |
|---|---|---|
| 1 | 4 oz (125 g) package low-fat cream cheese | 1 |
| ½ cup | low-fat ricotta cheese | 125 mL |
| ¼ cup | sugar | 50 mL |
| 1 tsp | vanilla extract | 5 mL |
| 3 | kiwis, peeled and sliced | 3 |
| 1 cup | berries, sliced (strawberries, raspberries, blueberries) | 250 mL |
| 1 cup | pineapple chunks (fresh or canned, unsweetened) | 250 mL |

## GLAZE

| | | |
|---|---|---|
| ⅔ cup | sugar | 150 mL |
| ½ tbsp | cornstarch | 7 mL |
| 1 cup | orange juice | 250 mL |

■ Preheat oven to 375 F (190 C). Spray a pizza pan or cookie sheet with nonstick cooking spray.

■ To prepare crust, combine first three ingredients. Add buttermilk and oil and mix with fork until dough forms ball. Flatten ball into a 4-inch (10.5 cm) circle and refrigerate in plastic wrap for 30 minutes.

■ On a flat surface, roll dough between sheets of wax paper to about ⅛-inch (.25 cm) thickness. Peel off top sheet and invert dough on pizza pan. Remove remaining wax paper. Bake in oven for approximately 12 minutes. Remove from oven and cool.

To make topping, mix cheeses, sugar, and vanilla until smooth. Spread on crust and decorate with fruit.

To prepare glaze, combine ingredients in a saucepan. Bring to boil over medium heat and cook for 1 minute, stirring constantly. Remove from heat and cool 5 minutes. Pour over fruit and refrigerate. Serve same day.

SERVES 8

PER SERVING
*315 calories*
*7.7 g fat*
*22% calories from fat*

# Cookies and Bars

### Exercise—Cycling

*Recapture one of your best childhood memories. Few of us will forget that first spin on our birthday bikes. The memory of that exhilarating feeling of freedom may be why so many grown-up kids are turning to cycling for their sporting activity.*

*Cycling is one of the best calorie burners around. An hour ride will expend up to 700 calories with very little stress on joints. Once you own a bike, riding is free and can be done just about anywhere.*

*The bicycle you buy has to fit your lifestyle. Should you buy a touring bike or a mountain bike? If the ten-speed is a Ferrari, the mountain bike is a Range Rover. One is built for speed, the other for endurance. A mountain bike is built to bash its way up steep, rocky trails or pot-holed city streets. It's built for adventure with upright handlebars, wide tires, and a fat frame, but if you want to ride like the wind, a racing bike may be your best choice. Designed for hurtling down long stretches of paved road, a racing bike is ideal if you plan to ride with a cycling club.*

*A bicycle is like a suit: it has to fit you. To find the right frame size, straddle the bike and stand with your feet flat. With a speed bike, you should clear the top tube by an inch or two. With a mountain bike, there should be as much as five inches clearance between*

# *Brownies*

*Did you know that cocoa powder is lower in fat than chocolate? Use cocoa instead of chocolate whenever you can in recipes and drinks. These brownies are fudgey and decadent without being fattening. What a concept! Serve with low-fat frozen yogurt or ice cream.*

NOTE: *This recipe is not the brownie manufactured and distributed for sale by Three Blondes and a Brownie Inc.*

| | | |
|---|---|---|
| 1 cup | all-purpose flour | 250 mL |
| 1 ⅔ cups | sugar | 400 mL |
| ¾ cup | unsweetened cocoa powder | 175 mL |
| ½ tsp | baking powder | 2 mL |
| 7 | egg whites | 7 |
| 1 cup | pureed prunes (try baby food prunes) | 250 mL |
| ¼ cup | buttermilk | 50 mL |
| 2 tsp | vanilla | 10 mL |
| ½ cup | mini, semisweet chocolate chips | 125 mL |

Preheat oven to 350 F (180 C). Lightly spray a 11 x 8 x 2-inch (28 x 20 x 5 cm) baking pan with nonstick cooking spray.

In a large bowl, stir together the flour, sugar, cocoa, and baking powder. Set mixture aside.

In another large bowl or food processor, beat egg whites until foamy. Add the prunes, buttermilk, and vanilla.

Add the flour mixture to the egg mixture and beat until thoroughly combined. Fold in the chocolate chips.

◾ Transfer the batter to the prepared pan. Bake about 30 minutes, or until the brownies just begin to pull away from the sides of the pan. Do not overbake. Cool completely on a wire rack and cut into bars.

MAKES 18

**PER SERVING (1 brownie)**
*160 calories*
*2.9 g fat*
*16% calories from fat*

*the top tube and your groin. Make sure the seat is the right height in order to reduce stress on your knees. When your foot is at the bottom of the down stroke, your knee should only be slightly bent. At the top stroke, your thigh should be parallel to the top tube.*

*With the right equipment and knowledge, you can safely peddle your calories away.*

## Children at Risk

# Almond Meringues

*These cookies are light as air and a delightful accompaniment to frozen desserts.*

| | | |
|---|---|---|
| 3 | large egg whites | 3 |
| ¼ tsp | cream of tartar | 1 mL |
| ¼ tsp | salt | 1 mL |
| 1 cup | sugar | 250 mL |
| ½ cup | blanched almonds, slivered | 125 mL |

Preheat oven to 250 F (120 C). Line two baking sheets with parchment paper, or spray with nonstick cooking spray and dust with flour. Shake off excess.

In a large mixing bowl, beat egg whites with an electric mixer until foamy. Add cream of tartar and salt. Beat until soft peaks are formed. Gradually add sugar, beating until stiff but not dry. Fold in the almonds.

Drop by the spoonful onto the prepared baking sheets. Bake on separate racks for 30 minutes, or until golden brown and firm to the touch. Reverse the pans halfway through to ensure even baking.

Transfer meringues to a rack and let cool. Prepared ahead, they can be stored in an airtight container for up to 1 week.

MAKES 24

---

**PER SERVING (1 meringue)**
*53 calories*
*2 g fat*
*34% calories from fat*

---

# Granola Power Bars

*Children love these granola power bars. They are a healthier alternative to commercial granola bars which are high in calories and fat.*

| | | |
|---|---|---|
| 1 cup | chocolate chips | 250 mL |
| 1 cup | butterscotch chips | 250 mL |
| 2 cups | miniature marshmallows | 500 mL |
| ⅓ cup | honey | 75 mL |
| 1 ¼ cup | uncooked oats | 300 mL |
| ½ cup | prunes, chopped | 125 mL |
| ¼ cup | dried apricots, chopped | 50 mL |
| ¼ cup | raisins | 50 mL |
| ½ cup | wheat germ | 125 mL |
| 1 cup | Grapenuts cereal | 250 mL |
| 1 cup | Rice Krispies cereal | 250 mL |

*lower the risk of cardiovascular disease." The American Academy of Pediatrics recommends that children engage in twenty to thirty minutes of vigorous exercise each day. Television and video games are poor substitutes for the healthy, physical and psychological contact parents, siblings, and friends provide while engaging in physical activity together.*

*Children older than two should not consume more than 30 percent of their daily calories from fat. Give your children a head start on good nutrition by exposing them to treats that are both healthy and delicious.*

▢ Melt chips together in a microwave or double boiler. Add marshmallows and honey and stir until melted. Make sure mixture is thoroughly blended. Combine remaining ingredients and add to chocolate mixture.

▢ Pour into a 9 x 13-inch (23 x 33 cm) pan that has been coated with nonstick cooking spray and pat down. Cool in refrigerator and cut into squares when ready to serve.

MAKES 36

---

PER SERVING (1 bar)
*105 calories*
*4 g fat*
*34% calories from fat*

---

Exercise—Too Much of a
Good Thing

Regular exercise is an integral
part of weight loss programs
and has many positive benefits.
It reduces high blood pressure,
prevents osteoporosis, lowers
cholesterol, and is a great stress
reliever. But those who train so
hard they end up injuring and
re-injuring themselves are usually obsessive about exercise and
run the risk of permanent
injury. Deterioration occurs
when you do not give your body
enough time to rest and rebuild.
Without enough rest and proper nutrition, you'll begin a down-
ward spiral of decreased perfor-
mance.

Avoid linking food and exercise. If you exercise regularly but
think you are not losing weight,
it's because you're adding muscle while losing fat. Muscle
weighs more than fat, so your
bathroom scale will not reflect
an improvement. Measure yourself using a measuring tape
instead of a weight scale. You'll
be sure to see fewer inches.

You do not need to punish
yourself with excessive exercise
or deprivation if you want to
lose weight permanently.
Reduce your fat intake and
exercise normally. Be patient
and remember that occasional
treats are part of a healthy
diet.

# Oatmeal Chocolate Chip Cookies

*Curl up in front of a fire with a glass of milk and oatmeal
chocolate chip cookies. These traditional favorites are still
irresistible when made the low–fat, low–calorie way.*

| ¾ cup | diet margarine | 175 mL |
|---|---|---|
| ¾ cup | brown sugar | 175 mL |
| ¼ cup | granulated sugar | 50 mL |
| 2 | egg whites | 2 |
| ¼ cup | molasses | 50 mL |
| 1 tsp | vanilla | 5 mL |
| 1 cup | all-purpose flour | 250 mL |
| 1 tsp | cinnamon | 5 mL |
| ½ tsp | baking soda | 2 mL |
| 3 cups | quick-cooking oats | 750 mL |
| ¾ cup | semisweet chocolate chips | 175 mL |

■ Preheat oven to 350 F (180 C).

■ Beat butter and sugars together. Add egg whites,
molasses, and vanilla. Beat until smooth. In a separate
bowl stir together flour, salt, cinnamon, baking soda,
and oats. Combine with butter mixture. Add chocolate
chips.

■ Drop rounded teaspoonfuls of dough 1 inch (2.5
cm) apart onto baking sheets sprayed with nonstick
cooking spray. Bake for 12 to 15 minutes.

MAKES 60

---

PER SERVING (1 cookie)
*60 calories*
*1.6 g fat*
*25% calories from fat*

---

# Gingerbread Cookies

*If Christmas wouldn't be Christmas without gingerbread cookies, don't despair. At only 78 calories and 1.7 grams fat per cookie, who can resist this recipe?*

| | | |
|---|---|---|
| 1 cup | diet margarine | 250 mL |
| 1 cup | sugar | 250 mL |
| 2 | egg whites | 2 |
| ¾ cup | molasses | 175 mL |
| 1 tbsp | vinegar | 15 mL |
| 4 ¾ cups | all-purpose flour | 1.175 L |
| 1 ½ tsp | baking soda | 7 mL |
| ½ tsp | salt | 2 mL |
| 1 tbsp | ground ginger | 15 mL |
| 1 ½ tsp | cinnamon | 7 mL |
| 1 ½ tsp | cloves | 7 mL |
| ½ tsp | nutmeg | 2 mL |

Preheat oven to 375 F (190 C).

In a large bowl, cream together margarine and sugar. Stir in egg whites, molasses, and vinegar. Mix dry ingredients together and add to margarine mixture. Chill for 3 hours.

Divide dough into 4 balls. Roll each ball out between 2 sheets of wax paper. Cut shapes with floured, Christmas cookie cutters. Place shapes on nonstick cookie sheets and bake for approximately 8 minutes, or until dough springs back when pressed with finger. Cool on a rack.

To decorate with icing, mix ½ cup (125 mL) icing sugar with a few drops of skim milk.

MAKES 60

---

PER SERVING (1 cookie)
*78 calories*
*1.7 g fat*
*19% calories from fat*

# Breads and Pastries

# Banana Whole Wheat Pancakes

*These pancakes are a nice change from traditional Saturday morning pancakes and have a fraction of the fat and calories. If you are trying to lose weight, better let the children keep the maple syrup at their end of the table. Syrup has over 200 calories in a 4 tablespoon (60 mL) serving. Cover your pancakes with fruit moistened with 1 tablespoon (15 mL) of syrup for flavor. Enjoy.*

| ⅔ cup | whole wheat flour | 150 mL |
| ⅔ cup | all-purpose flour | 150 mL |
| 1 tbsp | sugar | 15 mL |
| ¾ tsp | baking soda | 4 mL |
| 1 ½ cups | buttermilk | 375 mL |
| 1 tbsp | canola oil | 15 mL |
| 2 | medium bananas, diced | 2 |
| 2 | egg whites, beaten stiff | 2 |

In a large bowl, combine flours, sugar, and baking soda.

In a small bowl, combine buttermilk, oil, and banana. Pour into flour mixture and stir until just moistened. Lightly fold in beaten egg whites.

Spray griddle with nonstick cooking spray. Heat griddle over medium heat until a drop of water splashed in pan sizzles. Drop batter 2 tablespoons (25 mL) at a time onto hot griddle, spread into 3-inch (7.5 cm) circles.

Don't let pancakes touch each other. Turn when edges start to brown and bubbles appear on top of pancakes. Cook for 1 or 2 more minutes, or until second side is lightly browned. Serve immediately.

SERVES 6 (4 PANCAKES EACH)

---

PER PANCAKE
*25 calories*
*1 g fat*
*25% calories from fat*

---

## Breakfast—The Most Important Meal of the Day

You can bank your money but not your calories so you may as well spend them. If you think you can maintain or lose weight by skipping meals during the day and saving the calories for later, you may find yourself eating most of the day's energy needs in one meal, usually dinner. Known as calorie loading, eating a large meal tends to overwhelm the body with calories it does not need, and those extra calories are turned into body fat.

If you'd rather hit the snooze alarm than eat breakfast or run errands instead of eating lunch, you may be engaged in a lifestyle habit that will eventually catch up to you. If you are too busy to eat, consider this: The American Dietetic Association states that people who eat breakfast tend to burn more calories, not just in the morning but throughout the day. Skipping meals tends to lower metabolic rates.

## Cheese Popovers

*If the mere thought of baking bread overwhelms you, start with quick and easy popovers. These popovers are crispy and golden brown on the outside and moist on the inside. They deflate quickly, so serve them hot.*

| | | |
|---|---|---|
| ¼ cup | whole wheat flour | 50 mL |
| 1 cup | all-purpose flour | 250 mL |
| 3 tbsp | Parmesan cheese, grated | 45 mL |
| ¼ tsp | salt | 1 mL |
| 1 | egg, beaten | 1 |
| 3 | egg whites, beaten slightly until frothy | 3 |
| ½ cup | 2% milk | 125 mL |
| ½ cup | skim milk | 125 mL |

Preheat oven to 450 F (230 C).

Blend together both flours, cheese, and salt.

In a separate bowl, combine egg, egg whites, and milk. Gradually add flour mixture, stirring well.

Heat an 8-cup muffin tin in oven for 2 minutes. Remove from oven and coat with nonstick cooking spray. Divide batter evenly, filling each cup halfway.

Bake for 10 minutes. Reduce heat to 350 F (180 C) and bake for 25 minutes, or until golden brown. Remove popovers from muffin tin and serve immediately.

MAKES 8

---

PER SERVING (1 popover)
*105 calories*
*2.2 g fat*
*18% calories from fat*

---

# Tea Scones

*Plain or plump with raisins or blueberries, cooked on a griddle or baked in the oven, these are quick and easy to make. Scones are usually cut into triangles or diamond shapes. These are dropped from a spoon to ensure as little handling as possible. The result is a light-as-a-feather scone.*

| | | |
|---|---|---|
| 2 cups | all-purpose flour | 500 mL |
| ¼ cups | granulated sugar | 50 mL |
| 1 tbsp | granulated sugar (for topping) | 15 mL |
| 2 tsp | baking powder | 10 mL |
| ½ tsp | salt | 2 mL |
| 3 tbsp | unsalted butter | 45 mL |
| 1 ½ cups | buttermilk | 375 mL |
| 1 cup | fresh or frozen blueberries | 250 mL |
| | – OR – | |
| ⅓ cup | raisins | 75 mL |

Preheat oven to 350 F (180 C).

In a large bowl, stir together flour, sugar, baking powder, and salt. Blend in butter with a pastry blender until mixture resembles coarse crumbs. Stir in blueberries or raisins. Make a well in the center and gradually stir in buttermilk until just blended. Dough should be sticky.

Drop by the spoonful onto a baking sheet sprayed with nonstick cooking spray. Sprinkle tops with remaining sugar.

Bake in oven for 15 to 20 minutes, or until golden. Serve warm.

MAKES 14

PER SERVING (1 scone)
*109 calories*
*2.7 g fat*
*22% calories from fat*

## Scones

Is nothing sacred? The traditional scone of Scotland has been converted into health food! The rich, biscuit-like tea cake has been transformed into a low-calorie, fat-conscious treat thanks to buttermilk, a misunderstood and misnamed dairy product. Buttermilk actually contains no butter. It originally referred to the thick, butter-specked liquid left over after churning whole milk into butter. Most buttermilk today is made from skim or 1% milk. With only 99 calories and 2 grams of fat per cup, it has fewer calories and less fat than whole milk (which contains 150 calories and 8 grams of fat per cup). Buttermilk imparts a fluffy, moist texture to baked goods, allowing a reduction in the amount of butter, cream, sour cream, and whole milk traditionally used.

Scones are the hot breads of Scotland. The word scone is pronounced in the soft Scottish accent like "scaun." The name originally came from Perthshire where the kings of Scotland were crowned on the Stony of Destiny or Scone, now under the Coronation Throne in Westminster Abbey. Tradition has it that the stone was Jacob's Pillow.

# Blueberry Corn Muffins

*Stretch your food dollar by mixing up a batch of these delicious, low-fat muffins. They are great for breakfast.*

| | | |
|---|---|---|
| 1 cup | all-purpose flour | 250 mL |
| ¼ cup | whole wheat flour | 50 mL |
| ⅔ cup | yellow cornmeal | 150 mL |
| 1 tbsp | baking powder | 15 mL |
| 1 tsp | cinnamon | 5 mL |
| ¼ tsp | salt | 1 mL |
| 1 cup | fresh or frozen blueberries | 250 mL |
| 1 | egg | 1 |
| ⅔ cup | skim milk | 150 mL |
| ½ cup | honey | 125 mL |
| 3 tbsp | canola oil | 45 mL |
| 2 tsp | sugar | 10 mL |

■ Preheat oven to 400 F (200 C).

■ In a large bowl, stir together the flours, cornmeal, baking powder, cinnamon, and salt. Stir in blueberries.

■ In a separate bowl, lightly beat the egg. Add milk, honey, and oil and stir well. Add the liquid mixture to the dry ingredients. Stir just enough to blend.

■ Spray a 12-cup muffin tin with nonstick cooking spray. Divide the batter equally among muffin cups. Sprinkle tops with sugar.

■ Bake for 18 to 22 minutes, or until the muffins have risen and are golden. Turn out onto a wire rack to cool.

MAKES 12

---

PER SERVING (1 muffin)
*158 calories*
*4 g fat*
*22% calories from fat*

---

# Pumpkin Spice Muffins

*You can help yourself to seconds of these muffins and still not match the amount of fat in a traditional muffin.*

| | | |
|---|---|---|
| 1 ¾ cups | flour (whole wheat or white, unbleached) | 425 mL |
| 1 tsp | baking powder | 5 mL |
| ½ tsp | baking soda | 2 mL |
| ¼ tsp | salt | 1 mL |
| 1 tsp | ground cinnamon | 5 mL |
| ¾ cup | pumpkin, cooked, fresh or canned | 175 mL |
| ⅔ cup | low-fat buttermilk | 150 mL |
| 2 tbsp | canola oil | 25 mL |
| ½ cup | honey | 125 g |
| 2 | egg whites, lightly beaten | 2 |

Preheat oven to 400 F (200 C). Line a 12-cup muffin tin with muffin papers or spray with nonstick cooking spray.

In a large bowl, sift together flour, baking powder, baking soda, salt, and cinnamon.

In another bowl, stir together remaining ingredients. Combine contents of both bowls, stirring until just blended. Divide batter equally among muffin cups.

Bake 20 minutes, or until muffins are springy to touch and lightly browned.

MAKES 12

---

PER SERVING (1 muffin)

*136 calories*
*3 g fat*
*19% calories from fat*

---

## Understanding the Grain Game

If you banned bread from your diet because you think it's fattening, it's time to plug in the toaster. For years bread has been a misunderstood food. The truth is, a slice of bread is no more fattening than an apple. If you choose carefully, bread is rich in complex carbohydrates, vitamins, and minerals and is a low-fat source of fiber. It also contains about 1 gram of fat and approximately 60 to 90 calories per slice.

Understanding the grain game is important since bread ought to be a basic source of fiber in your diet. The amount of fiber in bread has nothing to do with color, texture, or how healthful the name sounds. Check the package for the ingredients list. In order for bread to contain as much fiber as possible, the first ingredient must be a whole grain such as whole wheat flour or whole rye, not wheat flour.

Look for bread with 2 or 3 grams of fiber per slice. Keep in mind that diet or light usually means thinner, smaller slices. High fiber and natural mean whatever the manufacturer prefers; the words have no legal definition.

# Zucchini Pecan Loaf

*This loaf packs up easily for picnics and social gatherings.*

| | | |
|---|---|---|
| 1 ½ cups | whole wheat flour | 375 mL |
| 1 ½ cups | all-purpose flour | 375 mL |
| 1 ½ cups | sugar | 375 mL |
| 1 tsp | cinnamon | 5 mL |
| ½ tsp | nutmeg | 2 mL |
| 1 tsp | baking soda | 5 mL |
| ¼ tsp | baking powder | 1 mL |
| 6 | egg whites | 6 |
| 1 cup | applesauce | 250 mL |
| ½ cup | buttermilk | 125 mL |
| 2 ½ cups | zucchini, grated | 625 mL |
| ⅓ cup | chopped pecans | 75 mL |

■ Preheat oven to 350 F (180 C).

■ In a large bowl, mix dry ingredients together. In a separate bowl, combine egg whites, applesauce, buttermilk, and zucchini. Add to dry ingredients and stir until blended.

■ Spray a Bundt or tube pan with nonstick cooking spray. Sprinkle pan with chopped pecans. Gently pour batter into pan and bake in oven for 45 minutes to 1 hour.

SERVES 12

PER SERVING
*267 calories*
*3.8 g fat*
*13 % calories from fat*

# Banana Loaf

*Don't throw out bananas once they are past their prime. If the thought of baking a fattening banana bread is the last temptation you need, try this version. It's a new approach to an old favorite.*

| | | |
|---|---|---|
| 3 tbsp | vegetable oil | 45 mL |
| 1 | large egg | 1 |
| 1 | egg white | 1 |
| 1 tsp | vanilla extract | 5 mL |
| ⅔ cup | brown sugar, packed | 150 mL |
| ⅓ cup | hot, strong-brewed coffee | 75 mL |
| 1 ½ cups | ripe bananas, mashed | 375 mL |
| 2 cups | all-purpose flour, sifted | 500 mL |
| 1 ½ tsp | baking powder | 7 mL |
| ¼ tsp | baking soda | 1 mL |
| ½ tsp | salt | 2 mL |
| 1 tsp | cinnamon | 5 mL |
| ¼ cup | walnuts, chopped (optional) | 50 mL |

Preheat oven to 350 F (180 C). Prepare a 9 x 5-inch (23 x 13 cm) loaf pan with nonstick cooking spray.

In a large bowl, beat together oil, eggs, and vanilla. In another bowl, dissolve brown sugar in coffee and add mashed bananas. Combine contents of both bowls.

Combine dry ingredients and nuts. Add to banana mixture and stir just enough to blend.

Pour batter into prepared pan and bake for approximately 1 hour, or until a toothpick inserted into the center comes out clean. Cool for 10 minutes. Invert onto a rack and let cool completely.

SERVES 12

---

PER SERVING
*180 calories*
*5.4 g fat*
*27% calories from fat*

# Apple Cinnamon Buns

*If you're one of those people who reserves fat- and calorie-laden cinnamon buns for your weekend treat, try these. They're irresistible any day of the week.*

### DOUGH

| | | |
|---|---|---|
| ½ cup | low-fat cottage cheese | 125 mL |
| 1 cup | skim milk | 250 mL |
| ⅓ cup | sugar | 75 mL |
| 2 tbsp | canola oil | 25 mL |
| ½ tsp | salt | 2 mL |
| 4 ½ to 5 cups | all-purpose flour | 675 to 750 g |
| 1 | package active dry yeast | 1 |
| 2 | large eggs | 2 |
| 1 | egg white | 1 |
| 1 tbsp | skim milk (for brushing dough) | 15 mL |

### FILLING

| | | |
|---|---|---|
| ½ cup | brown sugar | 125 mL |
| 1 | apple, finely diced | 1 |
| 1 tbsp | ground cinnamon | 15 mL |

### TOPPING

| | | |
|---|---|---|
| 1 ¼ cups | confectioner's sugar, sifted | 300 mL |
| 1 tsp | corn syrup | 5 mL |
| 1 ½ tbsp | skim milk | 20 mL |
| 1 tsp | vanilla extract | 5 mL |

Preheat oven to 375 F (190 C).

To prepare dough, place cottage cheese in a cheesecloth, gather into a ball, and squeeze out moisture. Cottage cheese should be reduced to about ¼ cup (50 mL) of solids. Press cheese through a sieve into a saucepan. Add milk, sugar, oil, and salt and heat until lukewarm.

In a large bowl, combine 2 ¼ cups (550 mL) flour and the yeast. Add milk mixture. Add slightly beaten eggs and beat with mixer on high speed for 3 minutes. Using a wooden spoon or dough hook, stir in as much of the remaining flour as possible.

Turn dough onto a lightly floured surface and knead for about 5 minutes, adding enough of remaining flour to make dough soft and smooth. Place in a lightly oiled bowl and turn once. Cover with plastic wrap and let rise in a warm place for approximately 1 hour, or until doubled in size.

Stir together filling ingredients.

### ASSEMBLY

Punch down dough and let rest, covered, on a slightly floured surface for 10 minutes.

Roll dough into a 12 x 18-inch (30 x 45 cm) rectangle.

Sprinkle filling over dough. Roll up into a jelly roll and slice into 12 pieces.

Place in a 9 x 13-inch (23 x 33 cm) pan coated with nonstick cooking spray. Cover with plastic wrap and let rise in a warm place for about 1 hour, or until doubled in size.

Brush with milk and bake in oven for 25 to 30 minutes.

Combine topping ingredients and drizzle over hot, baked rolls.

SERVES 12

---

### PER SERVING
*334 calories*
*4.8 g fat*
*12% calories from fat*

*such as olive oil and peanut oil, are the main fats used in countries like Japan and Italy where the rate of coronary disease is very low. Polyunsaturates include sunflower, corn, and soybean oils. These counter the cholesterol-raising effects of saturated fats. To sum it up, know your fats.*

# Apple Phyllo Strudel

*This uses the same phyllo pastry recipe used in the Spinach Cheese Strudel. It works beautifully with any recipe that calls for phyllo pastry, whether savory or sweet, and saves hundreds of fat calories.*

| | | |
|---|---|---|
| 1 | large egg white | 1 |
| 2 tbsp | olive oil | 25 mL |
| 6 | sheets phyllo pastry | 6 |
| 2 tbsp | fine, dry breadcrumbs | 25 mL |
| 6 | apples, peeled and sliced thinly | 6 |
| ½ cup | sugar | 125 mL |
| 1 tbsp | sugar (for topping) | 15 mL |
| ¼ cup | raisins | 50 mL |
| 2 tsp | cinnamon | 10 mL |

Preheat oven to 400 F (200 C). Lightly coat a baking sheet with nonstick cooking spray or line with parchment paper.

In a small bowl, whisk egg white with oil. Lay a sheet of phyllo on the work surface and, using a pastry brush, lightly coat the surface with the egg white mixture. Sprinkle with ½ tsp (2 mL) breadcrumbs. Repeat this step, layering more sheets of phyllo on top.

Mix apples, sugar, raisins, and cinnamon together. Pile the mixture in a row about 2 inches (5 cm) from the end of the phyllo pastry. Lift edges of dough nearest the apples and roll over to form a roll. Brush with remaining egg mixture, then sprinkle with 1 tbsp (5 mL) of sugar. Bake 20 to 25 minutes, or until pastry is golden brown.

SERVES 6

PER SERVING
*263 calories*
*3.8 g fat*
*13% calories from fat*

# *Measurement Conversion Chart*

| STANDARD | METRIC |
|---|---|
| ¼ tsp | 1 mL |
| ½ tsp | 2 mL |
| 1 tsp | 5 mL |
| | |
| 1 tbsp | 15 mL |
| 2 tbsp | 25 mL |
| | |
| ¼ cup | 50 mL |
| ⅓ cup | 75 mL |
| ½ cup | 125 mL |
| ⅔ cup | 150 mL |
| ¾ cup | 175 mL |
| 1 cup | 250 mL |
| 1 ½ cups | 375 mL |
| 2 cups | 500 mL |
| | |
| ¼ lb or 4 oz | 125 g |
| ½ lb or 8 oz | 250 g |
| ¾ lb or 12 oz | 375 g |
| 1 lb or 16 oz | 500 g |
| | |
| .39 in | 1 cm |
| 1 in | 2.54 cm |

# Fat Substitute Guide

| Instead of | Replace with | Calories Saved | Fat (g) Saved |
|---|---|---|---|
| **Snacks** | | | |
| 2 chocolate chip cookies | 3 ginger snaps or | 80 | 8 |
| | 2 fig bars or | 100 | 11 |
| | 4 graham crackers | 90 | 10 |
| 4.5 oz (125 g) cheesecake | 4.5 oz angel food cake | 300 | 32 |
| 4.5 oz (125 g) pecan pie | 4.5 oz lemon meringue | 170 | 12 |
| | or 4.5 oz pumpkin pie | 235 | 11 |
| 1 cup (250 g) vanilla ice cream | 1 cup vanilla frozen yogurt | 90 | 10 |
| 3 cups (750 g) buttered popcorn | 3 cups unbuttered popcorn | 216 | 24 |
| 3 cups (750 g) microwave popcorn | 3 cups microwave light popcorn | 100 | 7 |
| 2 oz (50 g) potato chips | 2 oz pretzels | 110 | 19 |
| 1 croissant | 1 bagel | 0 | 10 |
| 2 oz (50 g) caramels | 2 oz gummy bears | 50 | 5 |
| 2 oz (50 g) macadamia nuts | 2 oz roasted chestnuts | 175 | 30 |
| 1 pina colada cocktail | 1 Bloody Mary or | 160 | 3 |
| | 1 Martini | 160 | 3 |
| **Dairy Products** | | | |
| 1 cup (250 mL) whole milk | 1 cup skim milk | 64 | 8 |
| 1 cup (250 mL) 2% milk | 1 cup skim milk | 39 | 4 |

| | | | |
|---|---|---|---|
| 1 cup (250 mL) 2% milk | 1 cup buttermilk | 30 | 3 |
| 1 cup (250 mL) heavy cream | 1 cup evaporated skim milk | 620 | 87 |
| 1 cup (250 mL) sour cream | 1 cup nonfat sour cream or | 346 | 48 |
| | 1 cup nonfat plain yogurt | 366 | 48 |
| 8 oz (250 g) cream cheese | 8 oz light cream cheese or | 300 | 39 |
| | 8 oz nonfat cream cheese | 585 | 78 |
| 2 oz (50 g) ricotta cheese | 2 oz part skim ricotta cheese | 55 | 4 |
| 8 oz (250 g) Cheddar cheese | 8 oz reduced-fat Cheddar cheese | 341 | 50 |
| 8 oz (250 g) feta cheese | ½ feta cheese and ½ fat-free cottage cheese | 230 | 24 |
| 1 egg | 2 egg whites | 60 | 5 |

**Fats and Oils**

| | | | |
|---|---|---|---|
| 2 tbsp (25 mL) oil (for sautéing) | 2 tbsp chicken broth | 236 | 24 |
| ½ cup (125 mL) oil (for baking) | ½ cup unsweetened applesauce | 911 | 109 |
| 1 cup (250 g) butter or margarine (for icings) | 1 cup marshmallow cream | 784 | 184 |
| 1 tbsp (15 mL) butter or margarine | 1 ¼-second nonstick cooking spray | 98 | 10 |

### Meats and Fish

| | | | |
|---|---|---|---|
| 6 oz (170 g) can oil-packed tuna | 6 oz can water-packed tuna | 124 | 14 |
| roasted chicken breast with skin | chicken breast, skinless | 45 | 5 |
| 1 lb (500 g) ground beef | 1 lb lean ground beef or | 350 | 27 |
| | 1 lb ground chicken breast or | 767 | 73 |
| | 1 lb ground turkey breast | 852 | 90 |
| 3 oz (85 g) roast pork | 3 oz lean roast ham | 86 | 5 |
| 3 oz (85 g) mackerel or salmon | 3 oz sole, cod, halibut, or snapper | 90 | 9 |

### Miscellaneous

| | | | |
|---|---|---|---|
| 1 tbsp (15 mL) mayonnaise | 1 tbsp ultra-light mayonnaise or | 85 | 11.8 |
| | 1 tbsp reduced-fat mayonnaise or | 45 | 5 |
| | 1 tsp (5 mL) mustard or | 100 | 12 |
| | ½ reduced-fat mayonnaise and ½ nonfat plain yogurt | 100 | 10 |
| 1 oz (25 g) unsweetened chocolate | 3 tbsp (45 mL) unsweetened cocoa powder | 102 | 12 |
| 1 cup (250 mL) chocolate chips (for baking) | ¾ cup (175 mL) chocolate chips | 215 | 15 |
| 1 cup (250 mL) flaked coconut | 1 tsp (5 mL) coconut flavoring | 338 | 24 |

| | | | |
|---|---|---|---|
| 2 tbsp (25 mL) tartar sauce | 2 tbsp cocktail or seafood sauce | 170 | 18 |
| 1 cup (250 mL) milkshake | 1 cup McDonald's milkshake | 100 | 10 |
| 1 cup (250 mL) cream soup | 1 cup broth-based soup | 112 | 13 |
| 1 cup (250 mL) cranberry juice | 1 cup orange juice | 40 | 0 |

# Personal Fat Budget Guide

**F**AT—we feel compelled to add it to our diets. But the irony is that tasted by itself we probably wouldn't enjoy fat much. And unfortunately, fat appears almost instantly on places we really would like to keep trim.

The key to weight loss or maintaining a certain weight is to monitor fat intake. For instance, the average male (we know there really isn't such a creature) consumes about 2,700 calories daily while his female counterpart takes in about 1,900 calories.

Included in those calories (based on a 30 percent fat composition) are usually some 90 grams of fat in the man's diet and 65 grams in the woman's, but to lose weight or maintain a good physique, the fat grams should be reduced to 50 grams and 40 grams respectively, roughly 20 percent of daily food intake.

To help monitor fat intake, I've prepared this guide for you to use. It contains both prepared foods and recipe ingredients. At the end is a list of fast foods you might typically find in restaurants (fat grams only are listed). Think of allowing yourself a certain amount of fat grams each day, and just as you would not overdraw on your bank account (this is just hypothetical), do not spend more fat grams than your budget allows. It won't take long before you remember many of the items and are able to select your snack or meal knowing what you have left in your daily fat budget.

The information in this guide is adapted from the *Nutrient Value of Some Common Foods,* Health and Welfare Canada.

| ABBREVIATIONS AND SYMBOLS | |
|---|---|
| gram | g |
| milliliter | mL |
| centimeter | cm |
| diameter | diam |
| kilocalorie | kcal |
| none | 0 |
| trace | tr |
| Butter Fat | BF |

| FOOD | MEASURE | CALORIES (kcal) | FAT (g) |
|---|---|---|---|
| **DAIRY PRODUCTS** | | | |
| **Cheese** | | | |
| Blue | 45 g | 159 | 13 |
| Brick | 45 g | 167 | 13 |
| Camembert | 45 g | 135 | 11 |
| Cheddar | 45 g | 181 | 15 |
| Cheddar, grated | 7 g | 28 | 2 |
| Cottage, creamed 4.5% BF | 230 g | 238 | 10 |
| Cottage, 2% BF | 239 g | 214 | 5 |
| Cottage, dry curd, 0.4% BF | 153 g | 129 | tr |
| Cream | 15 g | 52 | 5 |
| Feta | 45 g | 123 | 10 |
| Gouda | 45 g | 164 | 13 |
| Gruyère | 45 g | 186 | 15 |
| Mozzarella | 45 g | 132 | 10 |
| Mozzarella, made with part skim milk | 45 g | 118 | 7 |
| Muenster | 45 g | 166 | 14 |
| Parmesan, grated | 5 g | 23 | 2 |
| Provolone | 45 g | 158 | 12 |
| Ricotta, made with part skim milk | 45 g | 62 | 4 |
| Ricotta, made with whole milk | 45 g | 78 | 6 |
| Swiss | 45 g | 169 | 12 |
| Processed spread, Cheddar | 15 g | 44 | 3 |
| Processed spread, made with skim milk | 15 g | 29 | tr |
| Processed food, Cheddar, cold pack | 45 g | 149 | 11 |
| Processed, Cheddar | 45 g | 169 | 14 |
| Processed, Cheddar, made with skim milk | 45 g | 86 | 3 |
| Processed Swiss | 45 g | 150 | 11 |
| **Cream** | | | |
| Cereal (half-and-half), 12% BF | 250 mL | 344 | 31 |
| Sour, 14% BF | 250 mL | 385 | 35 |
| Table (coffee), 18% BF | 15 mL | 28 | 3 |
| Whipped cream, pressurized | 15 mL | 10 | tr |
| Whipping, 35% BF | 250 mL | 822 | 88 |
| **Frozen Desserts** | | | |
| Ice cream, vanilla, hard, rich, 16% BF | 78 g | 184 | 12 |
| Ice cream, vanilla, hard, 10% BF | 70 g | 142 | 8 |

| Ice milk, vanilla, soft serve | 92 g | 129 | 4 |
| Sherbet, orange | 102 g | 143 | 2 |

### Imitation Cream Products

| Coffee whitener (nondairy), liquid, frozen | 15 mL | 20 | 1 |
| Coffee whitener (nondairy), powdered | 5 mL | 11 | tr |
| Dessert topping (nondairy), powdered and whole milk | 15 mL | 9 | tr |
| Dessert topping (nondairy), semisolid (frozen) | 15 mL | 16 | 1 |
| Dessert topping (nondairy), whipped, pressurized | 15 mL | 11 | tr |

### Milk Beverages

| Eggnog, commercial | 250 mL | 361 | 20 |
| Milk, chocolate, part skim, 2% BF | 250 mL | 189 | 5 |
| Milk, hot cocoa, made with whole milk | 250 mL | 230 | 10 |
| Milk, malted, made with whole milk | 250 mL | 250 | 11 |
| Milk, shake, chocolate, thick, commercial type | 250 mL | 250 | 6 |
| Milk, shake, vanilla, thick, commercial type | 250 mL | 231 | 6 |

### Milk Desserts

| Pudding mix, low calorie, prepared with skim milk | 137 g | 137 | 3 |
| Pudding, canned, chocolate | 132 g | 191 | 10 |
| Pudding, canned, vanilla | 132 g | 205 | 9 |
| Pudding, cornstarch, cooked | 137 g | 170 | 4 |
| Pudding, cornstarch, instant with whole milk | 137 g | 171 | 3 |
| Pudding, custard, baked | 140 g | 161 | 8 |
| Pudding, rice with raisins | 140 g | 204 | 4 |
| Pudding, tapioca (minute) | 87 g | 117 | 4 |

### Milk, Fluid

| Buttermilk | 250 mL | 105 | 2 |
| Goat, whole | 250 mL | 178 | 11 |
| Human, whole, mature | 250 mL | 181 | 11 |
| Part skim, 2% BF | 250 mL | 128 | 5 |
| Skim | 250 mL | 90 | tr |
| Soybean | 250 mL | 84 | 5 |
| Whole, 3.3% BF | 250 mL | 159 | 9 |

### Milk, Processed

| | | | |
|---|---|---|---|
| Condensed, sweetened, canned | 250 mL | 1036 | 28 |
| Dry, skim, powder, reconstituted (25 g yields 250 mL) | 25 g | 90 | tr |
| Dry, whole | 15 mL | 40 | 2 |
| Evaporated, whole, 7.8% BF, undiluted | 250 mL | 357 | 20 |
| Evaporated, 2% BF, undiluted | 250 mL | 246 | 5 |
| Evaporated, skim 0.3% BF, undiluted | 250 mL | 210 | tr |

### Yogurt

| | | | |
|---|---|---|---|
| Frozen, fruit, 6.3% BF | 125 g | 148 | 5 |
| Fruit flavor, 1.4% BF | 125 g | 131 | 2 |
| Plain, 1.5% BF | 125 g | 79 | 2 |

### Eggs

| | | | |
|---|---|---|---|
| Egg, large, fried in butter | 1 egg | 83 | 6 |
| Egg, large, raw or cooked in shell | 1 egg | 75 | 5 |
| Egg, large, scrambled, with milk and butter | 1 egg | 95 | 7 |
| Egg, white, large, raw or cooked in shell | 1 white | 16 | tr |
| Egg, yolk, large, raw or cooked in shell | 1 yolk | 63 | 6 |
| Egg substitute, frozen (yolk replaced) | 60 mL | 97 | 7 |

## MEAT, POULTRY, FISH, AND SHELLFISH

### Assorted Meat Products

| | | | |
|---|---|---|---|
| Bologna, beef and pork (11 x 0.2 cm) | 1 slice | 70 | 6 |
| Bologna, turkey (11 x 0.2 cm) | 1 slice | 44 | 3 |
| Creton | 15 mL | 59 | 5 |
| Ham, luncheon meat, sliced, packaged (11 x 11 x 0.2 cm) | 1 slice | 49 | 3 |
| Liverwurst | 15 mL | 49 | 4 |
| Salami, cooked, beef and pork (11 cm diam x 0.2 cm) | 1 slice | 55 | 4 |
| Salami, cooked, turkey (11 cm diam x 0.2 cm) | 1 slice | 43 | 3 |
| Salami, dry type (4.5 cm diam x 0.3 cm) | 1 slice | 25 | 2 |
| Sausages, beef and pork, cooked, 16 per 500 g pack | 1 sausage | 59 | 5 |
| Sausages, pork, cooked, 16 per 500 g pack | 1 sausage | 55 | 5 |
| Wieners, beef and pork, 12 per 450 g pack | 1 wiener | 118 | 11 |
| Wieners, chicken, 12 per 450 g pack | 1 wiener | 95 | 7 |
| Wieners, turkey, 12 per 450 g pack | 1 wiener | 84 | 7 |

### Beef

| | | | |
|---|---|---|---|
| Corned, brisket, cooked | 90 g | 226 | 17 |
| Corned, canned | 4 slices | 210 | 13 |
| Corned, hash with potatoes | 250 mL | 420 | 26 |
| Ground, lean, broiled, medium (8 cm diam x 1.5 cm) | 1 patty | 209 | 13 |
| Ground, regular, broiled, medium (8 cm diam x 1.5 cm) | 1 patty | 254 | 18 |
| Ground, regular, broiled, well done (8 cm diam x 1.5 cm) | 1 patty | 257 | 17 |
| Ground, regular, pan-fried, medium (8 cm diam x 1.5 cm) | 1 patty | 269 | 20 |
| Ground, regular, pan-fried, well done (8 cm diam x 1.5 cm) | 1 patty | 252 | 17 |
| Roast, blade, braised, lean and fat (11 x 6 x 0.6 cm) | 2 pieces | 249 | 16 |
| Lean only | 2 pieces | 216 | 11 |
| Roast, rib, roasted, lean and fat (11 x 6 x 0.6 cm) | 2 pieces | 256 | 18 |
| Lean only | 2 pieces | 196 | 10 |
| Roast, rump, roasted, lean and fat (11 x 6 x 0.6 cm) | 2 pieces | 205 | 10 |
| Lean only | 2 pieces | 177 | 7 |
| Steak, inside top round, broiled lean and fat (11 x 6 x 1.2 cm) | 1 piece | 154 | 5 |
| Lean only | 1 piece | 144 | 3 |
| Steak, sirloin, broiled lean and fat (11 x 6 x 1.2 cm) | 1 piece | 188 | 9 |
| Lean only | 1 piece | 163 | 6 |
| Stewing, simmered, lean only | 250 mL | 335 | 14 |

### Fish and Shellfish

| | | | |
|---|---|---|---|
| Anchovy | 3 fillets | 21 | 1 |
| Bluefish, baked or broiled (12 x 7 x 1 cm) | 1 piece | 146 | 5 |
| Clams, canned, drained solids | 7 clams | 82 | 2 |
| Cod, fresh, broiled with butter or margarine (10 x 4 x 2 cm) | 1 piece | 150 | 5 |
| Crab, canned, solids only | 150 mL | 87 | 2 |
| Fish sticks, breaded, frozen, cooked | 3 sticks | 158 | 8 |
| Haddock, breadcrumb, milk and egg coated, fried | 1 fillet | 182 | 7 |
| Halibut, broiled with butter or margarine (12 x 7 x 1 cm) | 1 piece | 157 | 6 |

| | | | |
|---|---|---|---|
| Herring, smoked, kippered (11 x 4 x 0.6 cm) | 1 fillet | 116 | 7 |
| Lobster, canned | 150 mL | 87 | 1 |
| Mackerel, canned, solids and liquid | 150 mL | 174 | 11 |
| Oysters, raw, meat only | 9 small | 59 | 2 |
| Perch, ocean, frozen, breaded, fried, reheated (17 x 5 x 1 cm) | 1 piece | 297 | 18 |
| Salmon, canned, solids and liquid | 150 mL | 193 | 12 |
| Salmon, fresh, broiled or baked with butter or margarine (12 x 7 x 1 cm) | 1 piece | 167 | 7 |
| Sardines, canned in oil, solids only | 7 medium | 171 | 9 |
| Scallops, steamed | 7 scallops | 101 | 1 |
| Shrimp, canned solids | 28 med | 104 | tr |
| Shrimp, French fried, batter dipped | 11 large | 198 | 10 |
| Sole, baked with lemon juice, with butter | 1 fillet | 127 | 6 |
| Sole, baked with lemon juice, with margarine | 1 fillet | 127 | 6 |
| Sole, baked with lemon juice, without added fat | 1 fillet | 85 | 1 |
| Trout, lake, broiled or baked (17 x 5 x 1 cm) | 1 piece | 201 | 13 |
| Tuna salad | 125 mL | 198 | 10 |
| Tuna, canned in oil, drained solids | 125 mL | 167 | 7 |
| Tuna, canned in water, drained solids | 125 mL | 135 | 1 |
| Whitefish, baked, stuffed (12 x 7 x 1 cm) | 1 piece | 198 | 13 |

**Lamb**

| | | | |
|---|---|---|---|
| Leg, roasted, lean and fat (11 x 6 x 0.6 cm) | 2 slices | 243 | 16 |
| Lean only | 2 slices | 162 | 6 |
| Loin chop, broiled, lean and fat | 1 chop | 424 | 35 |
| Lean only | 1 chop | 164 | 7 |
| Shoulder, roasted, lean and fat (7 x 6 x 0.6 cm) | 3 slices | 281 | 23 |
| Lean only | 3 slices | 170 | 8 |

**Organ and Glandular Meats**

| | | | |
|---|---|---|---|
| Heart, beef, simmered | 92 g | 161 | 5 |
| Kidney, beef, simmered | 89 g | 128 | 3 |
| Kidney, pork, braised | 89 g | 134 | 4 |
| Liver, beef, pan-fried (16 x 6 x 1 cm) | 1 piece | 187 | 7 |
| Liver, calf, fried (8 x 6 x 0.6 cm) | 3 slices | 248 | 13 |
| Liver, chicken, simmered | 5 livers | 157 | 5 |
| Liver, pork, braised (16 x 6 x 1 cm) | 1 slice | 142 | 4 |
| Sweetbreads (thymus), beef, braised | 1 slice | 287 | 22 |
| Tongue, beef, simmered | 90 g | 255 | 19 |

### Pork, Cured

| | | | |
|---|---|---|---|
| Bacon, back, sliced, grilled | 1 slice | 43 | 2 |
| Bacon, side, pan-fried, crisp | 2 slices | 75 | 6 |
| Ham, roasted lean and fat (11 x 6 x 0.6 cm) | 2 slices | 211 | 15 |
| Lean only | 2 slices | 128 | 5 |

### Pork, Fresh

| | | | |
|---|---|---|---|
| Leg, butt portion, roasted lean and fat (8 x 6 x 0.6 cm) | 2 slices | 233 | 14 |
| Lean only | 2 slices | 178 | 7 |
| Loin center cut chop, broiled, lean and fat | 1 chop | 263 | 18 |
| Lean only | 1 chop | 159 | 7 |
| Shoulder, whole, roasted, lean and fat (8 x 6 x 0.6 cm) | 3 slices | 257 | 18 |
| Lean only | 3 slices | 198 | 10 |
| Spareribs, braised, lean and fat | 2 medium | 235 | 18 |
| Tenderloin, roasted (4 x 4 x 1.5 cm) lean only | 3 slices | 148 | 4 |

### Poultry

| | | | |
|---|---|---|---|
| Chicken, broiler or fryer, roasted, breast meat only | 1/2 breast | 142 | 3 |
| Chicken, broiler or fryer, fried, breast meat plus skin, plus batter | 1/2 breast | 364 | 18 |
| Chicken, broiler or fryer, roasted, breast meat plus skin | 1/2 breast | 193 | 8 |
| Chicken, broiler or fryer, roasted, drumstick, meat only | 2 g | 151 | 5 |
| Chicken, canned, boned with broth | 87 g | 144 | 7 |
| Chicken, roasted, flesh only (7 x 5 x 0.6 cm) | 4 slices | 154 | 6 |
| Turkey roll, light and dark meat | 2 slices | 85 | 4 |
| Turkey, all classes, roasted dark meat | 2 slices | 161 | 6 |
| Light meat only | 2 slices | 135 | 3 |

### Veal

| | | | |
|---|---|---|---|
| Loin, cutlet or chop, broiled (7 x 6 x 2 cm) | 1 piece | 215 | 12 |
| Round with rump, broiled (11 x 6 x 0.6 cm) | 2 slices | 188 | 10 |

### Wild Game

| | | | |
|---|---|---|---|
| Bear, polar, flesh, simmered | 90 g | 163 | 4 |
| Beaver, roasted | 90 g | 223 | 12 |
| Caribou, cooked | 90 g | 157 | 1 |
| Hare or rabbit, cooked | 90 g | 194 | 9 |

| Moose, cooked | 90 g | 158 | 3 |
|---|---|---|---|
| Muskrat or porcupine, roasted | 90 g | 138 | 4 |
| Ptarmigan (grouse), roasted, meat only | 90 g | 156 | 5 |
| Seal, cooked | 90 g | 165 | 8 |

## LENTILS, NUTS, AND SEEDS

### Dry Beans

| Common, white, cooked, drained | 189 g | 263 | 1 |
|---|---|---|---|
| Lima, dry, cooked, drained | 199 g | 228 | 1 |
| Red kidney, cooked, drained | 187 g | 238 | 1 |
| Chickpeas (garbanzos), boiled, drained | 173 g | 284 | 4 |
| Lentils, cooked, drained | 209 g | 243 | 1 |
| Soybeans, mature seeds, cooked, drained | 182 g | 314 | 16 |
| Tofu (7 x 6 x 2 cm) | 89 g | 68 | 4 |

### Dry Peas

| Peas, split, cooked | 207 g | 244 | 1 |
|---|---|---|---|

### Nuts

| Almonds, shelled, whole | 75 g | 442 | 39 |
|---|---|---|---|
| Brazil nuts, raw | 74 g | 485 | 49 |
| Cashew nuts, roasted | 69 g | 397 | 33 |
| Coconut, dried, sweetened, shredded | 49 g | 245 | 17 |
| Nuts, mixed, dry roasted with peanuts | 72 g | 428 | 37 |
| Nuts, mixed, dry roasted with peanuts, salt added | 72 g | 428 | 37 |
| Nuts, mixed, oil roasted with peanuts, salt added | 75 g | 463 | 42 |
| Peanut butter, smooth, unsalted | 16 g | 95 | 8 |
| Peanut butter, smooth, salt added | 16 g | 95 | 8 |
| Peanuts, oil roasted | 76 g | 442 | 38 |
| Peanuts, oil roasted, salt added | 76 g | 442 | 38 |
| Pecans, halves | 57 g | 380 | 39 |
| Pistachio nuts, dry roasted, salt added | 68 g | 412 | 36 |
| Walnuts, English, chopped | 6 g | 39 | 4 |
| Walnuts, English, halves | 53 g | 340 | 33 |

### Seeds

| Pumpkin and squash, seed kernels, dry | 73 g | 395 | 33 |
|---|---|---|---|
| Sesame butter (tahini) from unroasted kernels | 14 g | 85 | 8 |

| | | | |
|---|---|---|---|
| Sesame seeds, dry | 79 g | 465 | 43 |
| Sunflower seed kernels, dry | 76 g | 433 | 38 |

**Vegetables and Related Products**

| | | | |
|---|---|---|---|
| Alfalfa seeds, sprouted with seed, raw | 35 g | 10 | tr |
| Asparagus, boiled, drained pieces | 190 g | 48 | tr |
| Asparagus, boiled, drained spears | 60 g | 15 | tr |
| Asparagus, canned, drained pieces | 256 g | 49 | 2 |
| Bamboo shoots, canned, drained solids | 138 g | 26 | tr |
| Bean sprouts, mung, boiled, drained | 131 g | 28 | tr |
| Bean sprouts, mung, stir-fried | 131 g | 66 | tr |
| Beans, lima, boiled, drained | 180 g | 221 | tr |
| Beans, snap, green, yellow or Italian, boiled, drained | 132 g | 46 | tr |
| Beans, snap, green, yellow or Italian, canned, drained | 144 g | 29 | tr |
| Beans, snap, green, yellow or Italian, frozen, boiled, drained | 144 g | 37 | tr |
| Beets, canned, sliced, drained | 180 g | 56 | tr |
| Beets, diced or sliced, boiled or drained | 180 g | 56 | tr |
| Beets, greens, boiled, drained | 152 g | 41 | tr |
| Broccoli, frozen, chopped, boiled, drained | 194 g | 54 | tr |
| Broccoli, raw, medium size | 151 g | 42 | tr |
| Broccoli, spears, boiled, drained | 165 g | 46 | tr |
| Broccoli, spears, whole stock, boiled, drained, medium size | 1 spear | 50 | tr |
| Brussels sprouts, boiled, drained | 165 g | 64 | tr |
| Brussels sprouts, frozen, boiled, drained | 165 g | 69 | tr |
| Cabbage, red, shredded, raw | 74 g | 20 | tr |
| Cabbage, shredded, boiled, drained | 158 g | 33 | tr |
| Cabbage, shredded, raw | 74 g | 18 | tr |
| Carrots, boiled, drained | 165 g | 74 | tr |
| Carrots, canned, drained | 154 g | 35 | tr |
| Carrots, frozen, boiled, drained | 154 g | 55 | tr |
| Carrots, raw (19 cm long) | 72 g | 31 | tr |
| Carrots, raw, shredded | 116 g | 50 | tr |
| Cauliflower, boiled, drained | 131 g | 31 | tr |
| Cauliflower, frozen, boiled, drained | 190 g | 36 | tr |
| Cauliflower, raw | 106 g | 25 | tr |
| Celery, diced, raw | 127 g | 20 | tr |
| Celery, outer stalk, raw (19 cm long) | 40 g | 6 | tr |
| Celery, pieces, boiled, drained | 158 g | 24 | tr |

| | | | |
|---|---|---|---|
| Chard, Swiss, boiled, drained | 185 g | 37 | tr |
| Coleslaw (cabbage salad) | 127 g | 88 | 3 |
| Corn, sweet, boiled, drained kernels | 77 g | 83 | tr |
| Corn, sweet, canned, cream style | 270 g | 194 | 1 |
| Corn, sweet, canned, kernels, drained | 173 g | 140 | 2 |
| Cucumber, raw, sliced | 111 g | 14 | tr |
| Eggplant, cubed, boiled, drained | 101 g | 28 | tr |
| Fiddlehead greens, frozen, cooked | 93 g | 19 | tr |
| Lettuce, iceberg, raw | 20 g | 3 | tr |
| Lettuce, loose leaf, shredded, raw | 59 g | 11 | tr |
| Mushrooms, boiled, drained | 48 g | 13 | tr |
| Mushrooms, canned, pieces, drained | 165 g | 40 | tr |
| Mushrooms, pieces, raw | 74 g | 19 | tr |
| Olives, black | 5 large | 26 | 3 |
| Olives, green | 5 med | 23 | 3 |
| Onion rings (breaded), frozen, heated in oven | 5 rings | 204 | 13 |
| Onions, chopped, boiled, drained | 222 g | 62 | tr |
| Onions, chopped, raw | 169 g | 57 | tr |
| Onions, frozen, chopped, boiled, drained | 222 g | 62 | tr |
| Onions, spring, chopped, raw | 6 g | 2 | tr |
| Parsley, chopped, raw | 4 g | 1 | tr |
| Parsnips, boiled, drained, slices | 165 g | 134 | tr |
| Peas (edible-podded), (Snow peas), boiled, drained | 169 g | 71 | tr |
| Peas (edible-podded), (Snow peas), raw | 153 g | 64 | tr |
| Peas, green, boiled, drained | 169 g | 142 | tr |
| Peas, green, canned, drained | 180 g | 124 | tr |
| Peas, green, frozen, boiled, drained | 169 g | 132 | tr |
| Peppers, hot, red, dried (chili) powder | 15 g | 47 | 3 |
| Peppers, sweet, green, boiled, drained | 1 pepper | 13 | tr |
| Peppers, sweet, green, raw | 1 pepper | 19 | tr |
| Pickles, assorted sweet | 1 piece | 12 | tr |
| Pickles, dill (10 cm long) | 1 dill | 15 | tr |
| Pickles, gherkins (7 cm long) | 1 piece | 29 | tr |
| Pickles, relish, sweet | 9 g | 12 | tr |
| Potato salad | 264 g | 378 | 22 |
| Potatoes, baked in skin, flesh and skin (12 cm long) | 1 potato | 225 | tr |
| Potatoes, baked in skin, flesh only (12 cm long) | 1 potato | 148 | tr |
| Potatoes, dehydrated flakes, prepared | 222 g | 251 | 12 |

| | | | |
|---|---|---|---|
| Potatoes, French fried, cooked in deep fat | 10 strips | 158 | 8 |
| Potatoes, French fried, frozen, heated | 10 strips | 111 | 4 |
| Potatoes, hashed brown, home prepared | 165 g | 252 | 23 |
| Potatoes, mashed, milk and butter added | 222 g | 235 | 9 |
| Potatoes, microwaved, flesh and skin (12 cm long) | 1 potato | 216 | tr |
| Potatoes, peeled before boiling (7 cm long) | 1 potato | 116 | tr |
| Potatoes, peeled after boiling (7 cm long) | 1 potato | 118 | tr |
| Potatoes, scalloped, dry mix, prepared | 259 g | 241 | 11 |
| Pumpkin, canned | 259 g | 88 | tr |
| Radishes, raw, without tops | 10 g | 8 | tr |
| Rutabagas, boiled, drained, cubed | 180 g | 61 | tr |
| Rutabagas, raw, cubed | 148 g | 53 | tr |
| Sauerkraut, canned, solids and liquids | 249 g | 47 | tr |
| Spinach, boiled, drained | 190 g | 44 | tr |
| Spinach, chopped, raw | 59 g | 13 | tr |
| Spinach, frozen, boiled, drained | 201 g | 56 | tr |
| Squash, summer, zucchini, boiled, drained | 190 g | 30 | tr |
| Squash, winter, butternut, frozen, boiled | 254 g | 99 | tr |
| Squash, winter, hubbard, boiled, mashed | 249 g | 75 | tr |
| Squash, winter, baked, cubes | 217 g | 85 | 1 |
| Sweet potatoes, candied (7 cm long) | 1 piece | 153 | 4 |
| Sweet potatoes, baked, peeled after baking (13 cm long) | 1 piece | 117 | tr |
| Sweet potatoes, boiled without skin, mashed | 346 g | 363 | 1 |
| Sweet potatoes, canned, vacuum-packed, mashed | 269 g | 245 | tr |
| Tomato juice, canned or bottled | 250 mL | 44 | tr |
| Tomato puree, canned | 50 mL | 22 | tr |
| Tomato sauce, canned | 50 mL | 16 | tr |
| Tomatoes, canned, stewed | 269 g | 70 | tr |
| Tomatoes, canned, whole | 254 g | 51 | tr |
| Tomatoes, raw | 1 medium | 23 | tr |
| Turnips, boiled, drained, mashed | 243 g | 44 | tr |
| Turnips, raw, cubed | 137 g | 37 | tr |
| Vegetable juice cocktail, canned | 250 mL | 49 | tr |
| Vegetables, mixed, canned, drained | 172 g | 81 | tr |
| Vegetables, mixed, frozen, boiled, drained | 172 g | 101 | tr |

## FRUITS AND RELATED PRODUCTS

### Fruits and Fruit Juices

| | | | |
|---|---|---|---|
| Apple juice, canned or bottled, vitamin C added | 250 mL | 123 | tr |
| Apple sauce, canned, sweetened | 250 mL | 204 | tr |
| Apple sauce, canned, unsweetened | 250 mL | 111 | tr |
| Apples, raw, with skin, medium size | 1 apple | 81 | tr |
| Apricot nectar, canned, vitamin C added | 250 mL | 148 | tr |
| Apricots, canned, whole, heavy syrup, no skin | 273 g | 227 | tr |
| Apricots, dried, cooked without sugar | 264 g | 224 | tr |
| Apricots, dried, uncooked | 137 g | 326 | tr |
| Apricots, dried, uncooked | 10 halves | 83 | tr |
| Apricots, raw | 1 whole | 17 | tr |
| Avocados, California (winter), raw | 1 whole | 306 | 30 |
| Avocados, Florida (summer/autumn), raw | 1 whole | 340 | 27 |
| Bananas, raw (22 cm long) | 1 piece | 105 | tr |
| Blackberries, raw | 152 g | 79 | tr |
| Blueberries, raw | 153 g | 86 | tr |
| Cantaloupe, raw, medium | 1/2 | 93 | tr |
| Cherries, sour, red, canned, water-packed | 258 g | 93 | tr |
| Cherries, sweet, raw | 153 g | 110 | 1 |
| Cranberries, whole, raw | 100 g | 49 | tr |
| Cranberry juice, cocktail, bottled | 250 mL | 155 | tr |
| Cranberry sauce, canned, sweetened | 250 mL | 442 | tr |
| Dates, pitted, chopped | 188 g | 517 | tr |
| Figs, dried, uncooked | 1 fig | 48 | tr |
| Fruit cocktail, canned, heavy syrup | 269 g | 196 | tr |
| Fruit cocktail, canned, juice-packed | 262 g | 121 | tr |
| Fruit cocktail, canned, water-packed | 259 g | 83 | tr |
| Fruit salad, tropical, canned | 272 g | 234 | tr |
| Grapefruit juice, canned, sweetened | 250 mL | 121 | tr |
| Grapefruit juice, canned, unsweetened | 250 mL | 99 | tr |
| Grapefruit juice, fresh | 250 mL | 102 | tr |
| Grapefruit juice, frozen, unsweetened, diluted | 250 mL | 107 | tr |
| Grapefruit juice, frozen, unsweetened, undiluted (335 mL can) | 1 can | 606 | 2 |
| Grapefruit, canned, syrup-packed | 268 g | 161 | tr |
| Grapefruit, pink and red, raw | 1/2 | 37 | tr |
| Grapefruit, white, raw | 1/2 | 39 | tr |

| | | | |
|---|---|---|---|
| Grapes, Canadian type (slip skin), raw | 10 g | 15 | tr |
| Grapes, European type (adherent skin), raw | 169 g | 120 | tr |
| Grapes, juice, canned or bottled | 250 mL | 163 | tr |
| Grapes, juice, frozen, sweetened, diluted, vitamin C added | 250 mL | 135 | tr |
| Grapes, juice, frozen, sweetened, undiluted, vitamin C added (170 mL can) | 1 can | 371 | tr |
| Honeydew melon, raw | 1/10 | 45 | tr |
| Kiwifruit, raw | 1 large | 56 | tr |
| Lemon juice, canned or bottled, unsweetened | 250 mL | 54 | tr |
| Lemon juice, fresh | 250 mL | 65 | 0 |
| Lemon, raw, without peel, medium size | 1 | 24 | tr |
| Lemonade, frozen concentrate, diluted | 250 mL | 115 | 0 |
| Lemonade, frozen concentrate, undiluted (355 mL can) | 1 can | 858 | tr |
| Lime juice, canned or bottled, unsweetened | 250 mL | 55 | tr |
| Lime juice, fresh | 250 mL | 70 | tr |
| Mangos, raw, peeled | 1 | 114 | tr |
| Nectarine, raw, peeled, medium size | 1 | 67 | tr |
| Orange juice, canned | 250 mL | 110 | tr |
| Orange juice, fresh | 250 mL | 118 | tr |
| Orange juice, frozen concentrate, diluted | 250 mL | 118 | tr |
| Orange juice, frozen concentrate, undiluted (170 mL can) | 1 can | 326 | tr |
| Orange-grapefruit juice, canned | 250 mL | 112 | tr |
| Oranges, raw, peeled, medium size | 1 | 62 | tr |
| Papayas, raw, peeled (9 cm diam x 13 cm) | 1 | 121 | tr |
| Peaches, canned halves or slices, heavy syrup | 270 g | 200 | tr |
| Peaches, canned halves or slices, juice-packed | 262 g | 115 | tr |
| Peaches, canned halves or slices, water-packed | 258 g | 62 | tr |
| Peaches, dried halves, cooked, no added sugar | 273 g | 210 | tr |
| Peaches, dried halves, uncooked | 169 g | 404 | 1 |
| Peaches, frozen, sliced sweetened | 340 g | 320 | tr |
| Peaches, raw, pared, whole, medium size | 87 g | 37 | tr |
| Peaches, raw, pared, sliced | 180 g | 77 | tr |
| Pears, canned halves or slices, heavy syrup | 269 g | 199 | tr |
| Pears, canned halves, juice-packed | 262 g | 131 | tr |
| Pears, raw, with skin, medium size | 169 g | 100 | tr |

| | | | |
|---|---|---|---|
| Pineapple juice, canned, vitamin C added | 250 mL | 148 | tr |
| Pineapple, canned cubes,water-packed | 260 g | 83 | tr |
| Pineapple, canned, heavy syrup, sliced (8 cm diam) | 64 g | 50 | tr |
| Pineapple, canned, heavy syrup, crushed | 269 g | 210 | tr |
| Pineapple, raw, diced | 164 g | 80 | tr |
| Plums, purple, canned, heavy syrup | 273 g | 243 | tr |
| Plums, raw, medium size | 66 g | 36 | tr |
| Prune juice, canned or bottled | 250 mL | 192 | tr |
| Prunes, dried, uncooked | 84 g | 201 | tr |
| Prunes, dried, cooked, without added sugar | 224 g | 240 | tr |
| Raisins, seedless | 174 g | 522 | tr |
| Raspberries, frozen, sweetened | 264 g | 272 | tr |
| Raspberries, raw | 130 g | 64 | tr |
| Rhubarb, frozen, cooked with added sugar | 254 g | 295 | tr |
| Rhubarb, raw, diced | 129 g | 27 | tr |
| Strawberries, frozen, sweetened, sliced | 269 g | 258 | tr |
| Strawberries, frozen, sweetened, whole | 269 g | 210 | tr |
| Strawberries, frozen, unsweetened | 157 g | 55 | tr |
| Strawberries, raw, hulled | 157 g | 47 | tr |
| Tangerines (mandarins), raw, medium size | 1 | 37 | tr |
| Tangerines (mandarins), canned, light syrup | 266 g | 162 | tr |
| Watermelon, raw (25 cm diam x 2 cm) | 1 slice | 118 | 2 |

## Fruit-Flavored Drinks

| | | | |
|---|---|---|---|
| Fruit-flavored drinks, canned or bottled, vitamin C added | 250 mL | 123 | 0 |
| Fruit-flavored drinks, crystals, water and vitamin C added | 250 mL | 102 | 0 |

## BREAD, CEREALS, AND RELATED PRODUCTS

### Biscuits and Crackers

| | | | |
|---|---|---|---|
| Biscuits, baking powder (5 x 3 cm) | 1 | 103 | 5 |
| Crackers, cheese | 4 round | 67 | 3 |
| Crackers, graham | 4 squares | 108 | 3 |
| Crackers, saltines (soda) | 4 squares | 48 | 1 |
| Crackers, snack type | 1 round | 15 | 1 |
| Crackers, wheat thin | 4 | 35 | 1 |
| Crackers, whole wheat wafers | 2 | 35 | 2 |

### Breads, Rolls, and Buns

| | | | |
|---|---|---|---|
| Bagels (9 cm diam) | 1 | 200 | 2 |
| Bread, cracked wheat | 1 slice | 66 | tr |
| Bread, French or Vienna | 1 slice | 58 | tr |
| Bread, Italian | 1 slice | 83 | tr |
| Bread, melba toast | 1 piece | 16 | tr |
| Bread, mixed grain | 1 slice | 65 | tr |
| Bread, oatmeal | 1 slice | 65 | 1 |
| Bread, pita (16.5 cm diam) | 1 | 165 | 1 |
| Bread, raisin | 1 slice | 66 | tr |
| Bread, rye, dark, pumpernickel | 1 slice | 79 | tr |
| Bread, rye, light | 1 slice | 61 | tr |
| Bread, white | 1 slice | 76 | tr |
| Bread, white, calcium carbonate added to flour | 1 slice | 76 | tr |
| Bread, whole wheat (100% whole wheat) | 1 slice | 61 | tr |
| Bread, whole wheat (60% whole wheat) | 1 slice | 63 | 1 |
| Breadcrumbs, white bread, dry | 106 | 416 | 5 |
| Buns, hamburger | 1 bun | 179 | 3 |
| Buns, hot dog | 1 bun | 149 | 3 |
| Croissants | 1 | 235 | 12 |
| English muffins | 1 | 140 | 1 |
| English muffins, toasted | 1 | 140 | 1 |
| Rolls, commercial, hard | 1 round | 156 | 2 |
| Tortillas, corn | 1 tortilla | 65 | 1 |

### Breakfast Cereals

| | | | |
|---|---|---|---|
| Bran flakes with raisins | 42 g | 133 | tr |
| Bran flakes, whole wheat | 40 g | 139 | tr |
| Bran, all bran | 45 g | 113 | tr |
| Bran, bran buds | 44 g | 122 | tr |
| Bran, 100% | 35 g | 90 | tr |
| Corn bran | 30 g | 118 | 1 |
| Corn flakes, plain | 19 g | 70 | tr |
| Corn flakes, sugar coated (Frosted Flakes) | 30 g | 114 | tr |
| Corn and oats (Cap'n Crunch) | 39 g | 154 | 2 |
| Corn and wheat, oats (Froot Loops) | 24 g | 93 | tr |
| Corn, puffed, presweetened (Sugar Corn Pops) | 30 g | 114 | tr |
| Granola, homemade | 64 g | 312 | 17 |
| Oatmeal, regular or quick cooking, cooked | 124 g | 77 | 1 |
| Oatmeal, regular or quick cooking, dry | 43 g | 165 | 3 |
| Oatmeal, ready to serve, dry | 32 g | 120 | 2 |

| | | | |
|---|---|---|---|
| Oats and marshmallows (Lucky Charms) | 34 g | 134 | tr |
| Oats, puffed (Cheerios) | 24 g | 92 | 2 |
| Oats, puffed, presweetened (Alpha Bits) | 30 g | 118 | tr |
| Red River, cooked | 125 g | 82 | tr |
| Rice Flakes | 27 g | 103 | tr |
| Rice Krispies | 30 g | 112 | tr |
| Rice and wheat (Special K) | 22 g | 82 | tr |
| Rice, puffed | 15 g | 59 | tr |
| Wheat, flakes (Grapenuts) | 27 g | 97 | tr |
| Wheat, flakes (Wheaties) | 24 g | 86 | tr |
| Wheat, puffed | 13 g | 50 | tr |
| Wheat, puffed, presweetened (Sugar Crisp) | 35 g | 132 | tr |
| Wheat to be cooked, enriched, cooked | 133 g | 68 | tr |
| Wheat, whole (Shredded Wheat) | 1 biscuit | 95 | tr |
| Wheat, whole (Shreddies) | 44 g | 169 | tr |

## CAKES

### Cake (from mix)

| | | | |
|---|---|---|---|
| Angel food cake (1/12 of 25 cm diam cake) | 1 piece | 137 | tr |
| Cupcakes (7 cm diam) | 1 | 116 | 4 |
| Gingerbread (1/9 of 21 cm square cake) | 1 piece | 174 | 4 |
| Coffee cake | 1/6 of cake | 232 | 7 |
| Devil's Food with icing (1/16 of 23 cm diam cake) | 1 piece | 234 | 8 |
| White layer with chocolate icing (1/16 of 23 cm diam cake) | 1 piece | 249 | 8 |

### Cake (home recipe)

| | | | |
|---|---|---|---|
| Boston Cream Pie (1/12 of 20 cm diam cake) | 1 piece | 208 | 6 |
| Carrot with cream cheese frosting | 1/8 cake | 241 | 13 |
| Fruitcake, dark (4 x 7.5 x 2 cm) | 1 slice | 227 | 9 |
| Pound cake (9 x 8 x 1 cm) | 1 slice | 142 | 9 |
| Sponge (1/12 of 22 cm diam cake) | 1 piece | 131 | 3 |
| White with boiled white icing (8 x 9 x 5 cm) | 1 piece | 401 | 12 |
| White plain (8 x 8 x 5 cm) | 1 piece | 313 | 12 |
| Yellow layer with chocolate icing (1/16 of 23 cm diam cake) | 1 piece | 274 | 10 |

| | | | |
|---|---|---|---|
| Yellow layer, no icing (1/16 of 23 cm diam cake) | 1 piece | 196 | 7 |
| Cheesecake (1/12 of 23 cm diam cake) | 1 piece | 278 | 18 |

### Cookies

| | | | |
|---|---|---|---|
| Brownies with nuts, home recipe | 1 brownie | 97 | 6 |
| Chocolate chip, commercial (6 cm diam) | 2 cookies | 104 | 5 |
| Chocolate chip, home recipe (6 cm diam) | 2 cookies | 103 | 6 |
| Chocolate marshmallow (Mallows) | 1 biscuit | 70 | 2 |
| Fig bars | 2 bars | 100 | 2 |
| Oatmeal with raisins | 2 cookies | 117 | 4 |
| Peanut butter, home recipe | 2 cookies | 123 | 7 |
| Sandwich, chocolate or vanilla, commercial | 2 round | 99 | 5 |
| Shortbread, commercial | 2 large | 139 | 6 |
| Shortbread, home recipe (margarine) | 2 large | 145 | 8 |
| Social Tea or Arrowroot | 2 biscuits | 57 | 2 |
| Sugar, from refrigerated dough | 2 cookies | 118 | 6 |
| Vanilla wafers | 5 cookies | 93 | 4 |

### Flours and Grains

| | | | |
|---|---|---|---|
| Barley, pearled, light, uncooked | 106 g | 370 | 1 |
| Bulgur | 185 g | 655 | 3 |
| Carob, flour | 148 g | 266 | 2 |
| Cornmeal, degermed, dry form | 73 g | 266 | tr |
| Cornstarch | 68 g | 246 | 0 |
| Potato flour | 189 g | 664 | 2 |
| Rice, brown, cooked | 180 g | 214 | 1 |
| Rice, white, short grain, cooked | 185 g | 202 | tr |
| Rice, white, short grain, raw | 211 g | 766 | tr |
| Rice, white, instant, ready-to-serve, cooked with butter and salt | 209 g | 255 | 4 |
| Rice, white, long-grain, parboiled, cooked | 169 g | 179 | tr |
| Rye, flour, light | 100 g | 357 | 1 |
| Soybean, flour, defatted | 106 g | 346 | tr |
| Wheat bran | 3 g | 6 | tr |
| Wheat germ | 7 g | 25 | tr |
| Wheat, flour, all-purpose | 133 g | 484 | 1 |
| Wheat, flour, all-purpose calcium carbonate | 133 g | 484 | 1 |
| Wheat, flour, cake | 114 g | 415 | 1 |
| Wheat, flour, whole | 127 g | 423 | 3 |

## Muffins

| | | | |
|---|---|---|---|
| Blueberry, home recipe, medium size | 1 | 312 | 12 |
| Bran, home recipe, medium size | 1 | 304 | 14 |
| Corn, made from mix with milk and eggs, medium size | 1 | 330 | 12 |
| Plain, home recipe, medium size | 1 | 318 | 14 |

## Pancakes and Waffles

| | | | |
|---|---|---|---|
| Buckwheat, made from mix with milk and eggs (10.2 cm diam) | 1 | 54 | 2 |
| Plain, made from mix with milk and eggs (10.2 cm diam) | 1 | 61 | 2 |
| Waffles, made from mix with milk and eggs | 1 round | 206 | 8 |

## Pasta

| | | | |
|---|---|---|---|
| Macaroni, enriched, cooked | 148 g | 164 | 1 |
| Noodles, chow mein, canned | 47 g | 230 | 11 |
| Noodles, egg, enriched, cooked | 169 g | 211 | 2 |
| Spaghetti, enriched, cooked | 148 g | 164 | 1 |

## Pies

*(one sector is 1/6 of 23 cm diam pie)*

| | | | |
|---|---|---|---|
| Apple, 2 crust | 1 sector | 404 | 18 |
| Blueberry, 2 crust | 1 sector | 382 | 17 |
| Cherry, 2 crust | 1 sector | 412 | 18 |
| Custard, 1 crust | 1 sector | 331 | 17 |
| Lemon meringue, 1 crust | 1 sector | 357 | 14 |
| Mincemeat, 2 crust | 1 sector | 428 | 18 |
| Peach, 2 crust | 1 sector | 403 | 17 |
| Pumpkin, 1 crust | 1 sector | 321 | 17 |
| Raisin, 2 crust | 1 sector | 427 | 17 |
| Pie crust, baked shell (23 cm diam) | 1 | 900 | 60 |
| Pies, fried, fast food apple | 1 pie | 255 | 14 |
| Pies, fried, fast food cherry | 1 pie | 250 | 14 |

## Snack Foods

| | | | |
|---|---|---|---|
| Cone for ice cream | 1 cone | 15 | tr |
| Popcorn, air popped, plain | 8 g | 31 | tr |
| Popcorn, popped with oil and salt | 12 g | 55 | 3 |
| Popcorn, sugar coated | 37 g | 142 | 1 |
| Potato chips | 10 chips | 105 | 7 |
| Pretzels, bread stick | 5 pretzels | 59 | tr |

| | | | |
|---|---|---|---|
| Pretzels, 3 ring | 1 | 12 | tr |

**Sweet Baked Goods**

| | | | |
|---|---|---|---|
| Danish pastry, plain, round (11 x 2.5 cm) | 1 | 274 | 15 |
| Date squares | 1 | 226 | 5 |
| Doughnuts, cake type | 1 | 168 | 10 |
| Doughnuts, yeast-leavened | 1 | 174 | 11 |
| Eclairs, chocolate, custard filled | 1 | 239 | 14 |

**Combination Dishes**

| | | | |
|---|---|---|---|
| Beans and wieners, canned | 272 g | 386 | 18 |
| Beans with tomato sauce and pork, canned | 267 g | 262 | 3 |
| Beef and vegetable stew, canned | 259 g | 205 | 8 |
| Beef pot pie, baked | 1/3 pie | 517 | 30 |
| Cheeseburger, regular, 2 oz patty | 1 | 300 | 15 |
| Cheeseburger, 4 oz patty | 1 | 525 | 31 |
| Chicken à la King, home recipe | 259 g | 495 | 36 |
| Chicken and noodles, home recipe | 254 g | 389 | 20 |
| Chicken pot pie, baked | 1/3 pie | 545 | 31 |
| Chili con carne without beans, canned | 269 g | 538 | 40 |
| Chili con carne with beans, canned | 269 g | 302 | 15 |
| Chop suey with meat or chicken | 264 g | 317 | 18 |
| Chow mein, chicken, canned, without noodles | 264 g | 100 | tr |
| Chow mein, chicken, home recipe, without noodles | 264 g | 269 | 11 |
| English muffin, egg, cheese and bacon | 1 | 360 | 18 |
| Fish cakes, fried (6.5 x 2 cm) | 1 | 103 | 5 |
| Fish sandwich, large, without cheese, fast food | 1 | 470 | 27 |
| Fish sandwich, regular, with cheese, fast food | 1 | 420 | 23 |
| Hamburger, regular, 2 oz patty | 1 | 245 | 11 |
| Hamburger, 4 oz patty | 1 | 445 | 21 |
| Luncheon meat, canned (8 x 5 x 1 cm) | 1 slice | 150 | 14 |
| Macaroni and cheese, canned | 254 g | 241 | 10 |
| Macaroni and cheese, home recipe | 211 g | 454 | 23 |
| Meat loaf, homemade (10 x 8 x 1 cm) | 1 slice | 117 | 6 |
| Pizza, cheese (1/8 of 35 cm diam) | 1 sector | 153 | 5 |
| Pizza, sausage (1/8 of 35 cm diam) | 1 sector | 183 | 9 |
| Quiche Lorraine (1/8 of 20 cm diam) | 1 sector | 600 | 48 |
| Roast beef sandwich, fast food | 1 | 345 | 13 |

| | | | |
|---|---|---|---|
| Spaghetti, with meat balls/tomato sauce, homemade | 262 g | 351 | 12 |
| Spaghetti, with tomato sauce and cheese, canned | 264 g | 201 | 2 |
| Taco, fast food | 1 taco | 195 | 11 |
| Tourtière (pork pie) (1/6 of 23 cm diam) | 1 sector | 482 | 30 |

## FATS AND OILS

### Butter

| | | | |
|---|---|---|---|
| Cup | 250 mL | 1720 | 195 |
| Tablespoon | 15 mL | 100 | 11 |
| Pat | 5 mL | 36 | 4 |

### Cooking Fats

| | | | |
|---|---|---|---|
| Lard | 250 mL | 1957 | 217 |
| Lard | 15 mL | 117 | 13 |
| Shortening, vegetable oil | 250 mL | 1953 | 217 |
| Shortening, vegetable oil | 15 mL | 117 | 13 |

### Margarine

| | | | |
|---|---|---|---|
| Tub: Vegetable oils, | | | |
|     no declaration of fatty acids | 250 mL | 1719 | 193 |
|     no declaration of fatty acids | 15 mL | 100 | 11 |
|     with declaration of fatty acids | 250 mL | 1719 | 193 |
|     with declaration of fatty acids | 15 mL | 100 | 11 |

### Oils

| | | | |
|---|---|---|---|
| Canola (rapeseed, colza) | 250 mL | 2033 | 230 |
| Canola (rapeseed, colza) | 15 mL | 124 | 14 |
| Corn | 250 mL | 2033 | 230 |
| Corn | 15 mL | 124 | 14 |
| Olive | 250 mL | 2033 | 230 |
| Olive | 15 mL | 124 | 14 |
| Peanut | 250 mL | 2016 | 228 |
| Peanut | 15 mL | 124 | 14 |
| Soybean | 250 mL | 2033 | 230 |
| Soybean | 15 mL | 124 | 14 |
| Sunflower | 250 mL | 2033 | 230 |
| Sunflower | 15 mL | 124 | 14 |

### Salad Dressings

| | | | |
|---|---|---|---|
| Mayonnaise, more than 65% oil | 15 mL | 102 | 11 |
| Mayonnaise type, more than 35% oil | 15 mL | 58 | 5 |
| Thousand Island, commercial | 15 mL | 64 | 6 |
| Blue cheese | 15 mL | 77 | 8 |
| French: | | | |
|     Calorie reduced, commercial | 15 mL | 24 | 2 |
|     Regular, commercial | 15 mL | 64 | 6 |
|     Home cooked, boiled | 15 mL | 25 | 2 |

## SUGAR AND SWEETS

### Candy

| | | | |
|---|---|---|---|
| Caramels, plain or chocolate | 3 | 120 | 3 |
| Chocolate-coated peanuts | 15 pieces | 168 | 12 |
| Chocolate fudge (3 x 3 x 2.5 cm) | 1 | 116 | 4 |
| Gum drops | 5 drops | 104 | tr |
| Hard candy | 6 | 116 | tr |
| Jelly beans | 10 beans | 110 | tr |
| Licorice | 3 sticks | 104 | tr |
| Marshmallows | 4 | 89 | 0 |
| Mints or fondant | 30 | 109 | tr |
| Chocolate, baking, bitter | 1 square | 141 | 15 |
| Chocolate, baking, sweet | 1 square | 148 | 10 |
| Gum, chewing | 1 stick | 13 | 0 |

### Chocolate-Flavored Beverage Powder

| | | | |
|---|---|---|---|
| With skim milk powder, made with water | 250 mL | 145 | 2 |
| Without milk powder, made with whole milk | 250 mL | 238 | 9 |

### Chocolate-Flavored Syrup

| | | | |
|---|---|---|---|
| Fudge type | 15 mL | 63 | 3 |
| Thin type | 15 mL | 47 | tr |

### Icings

| | | | |
|---|---|---|---|
| Chocolate, made with milk and fat | 250 mL | 1094 | 40 |
| Creamy fudge, from mix made with water | 250 mL | 878 | 17 |
| White, boiled | 250 mL | 313 | 0 |

**Other**

| | | | |
|---|---|---|---|
| Popsicle | 1 | 61 | 0 |

**Spreads**

| | | | |
|---|---|---|---|
| Honey, strained, liquid | 15 mL | 64 | 0 |
| Jams and preserves | 15 mL | 54 | tr |
| Jellies | 15 mL | 52 | tr |
| Molasses, blackstrap or cooking | 15 mL | 45 | 0 |
| Molasses, fancy (usually consumed) | 15 mL | 53 | 0 |

**Sugars**

| | | | |
|---|---|---|---|
| Brown | 232 g | 865 | 0 |
| Brown | 9 g | 34 | 0 |
| White, granulated | 211 g | 812 | 0 |
| White, granulated | 13 g | 50 | 0 |
| White, powdered | 127 g | 489 | 0 |

**Syrups**

| | | | |
|---|---|---|---|
| Maple | 15 mL | 50 | 0 |
| Table (blends) | 15 mL | 61 | 0 |

## MISCELLANEOUS ITEMS

**Alcoholic Beverages**

| | | | |
|---|---|---|---|
| Beer | 341 mL | 151 | 0 |
| Liquor (gin, rum, vodka, whiskey) | 50 mL | 109 | 0 |
| Dessert wine | 100 mL | 155 | 0 |
| Red table wine | 100 mL | 72 | 0 |
| White table wine | 100 mL | 68 | 0 |

**Nonalcoholic Beverages**

| | | | |
|---|---|---|---|
| Coffee | 250 mL | 5 | 0 |
| Soft drinks, club soda (soda water) | 280 mL | 0 | 0 |
| Soft drinks, cola type beverage | 280 mL | 120 | 0 |
| Soft drinks, cola type beverage with aspartame | 280 mL | 3 | 0 |
| Soft drinks, ginger ale | 280 mL | 98 | 0 |
| Soft drinks, tonic water | 280 mL | 98 | 0 |
| Tea, beverage | 250 mL | 3 | 0 |
| Tea, beverage, made from sweetened instant powder | 250 mL | 93 | 0 |

### Condiments

| | | | |
|---|---|---|---|
| Bouillon cubes | 1 cube | 10 | tr |
| Ketchup | 15 mL | 18 | tr |
| Mustard, prepared yellow | 15 mL | 12 | tr |
| Salt, table | 6 | 0 | 0 |
| Shake and bake, dry | 6 | 24 | tr |
| Vinegar, white | 15 mL | 2 | 0 |

### Gelatin

| | | | |
|---|---|---|---|
| Dessert powder | 1 package | 315 | 0 |
| Dessert, dietetic, prepared with water | 127 g | 10 | tr |
| Dessert, prepared with water | 127 g | 75 | 0 |
| Dry powder | 1 envelope | 23 | tr |

### Sauces and Gravy

| | | | |
|---|---|---|---|
| Barbecue sauce | 250 mL | 198 | 5 |
| Gravy, brown, canned | 15 mL | 8 | tr |
| White sauce, medium | 250 mL | 428 | 33 |

### Soups (canned, condensed)

| | | | |
|---|---|---|---|
| Bean with bacon, with water added | 250 mL | 182 | 6 |
| Beef broth, bouillon/consommé, with water added | 250 mL | 31 | 0 |
| Beef noodle, with water added | 250 mL | 88 | 3 |
| Clam chowder, Manhattan, with tomato, water added | 250 mL | 83 | 2 |
| Clam chowder, without tomato, with whole milk added | 250 mL | 173 | 7 |
| Cream of mushroom, with water added | 250 mL | 137 | 9 |
| Cream of mushroom, with whole milk added | 250 mL | 215 | 14 |
| Cream of chicken, with water added | 250 mL | 124 | 8 |
| Cream of chicken, with whole milk added | 250 mL | 202 | 12 |
| Minestrone, with water added | 250 mL | 87 | 3 |
| Split pea with ham, with water added | 250 mL | 200 | 5 |
| Tomato, with water added | 250 mL | 90 | 2 |
| Tomato, with whole milk added | 250 mL | 170 | 6 |
| Vegetable beef, with water added | 250 mL | 83 | 2 |
| Vegetable, vegetarian with water added | 250 mL | 77 | 2 |

### Soups (dehydrated dry form, prepared with water)

| | | | |
|---|---|---|---|
| Chicken noodle | 250 mL | 56 | 1 |
| Onion | 250 mL | 29 | tr |
| Tomato vegetable | 250 mL | 59 | tr |

## FAST FOOD

| FOOD | FAT (G) | | |
|---|---|---|---|

**Arby's**

| | |
|---|---|
| Club sandwich | 30.0 |
| Ham and cheese sandwich | 17.0 |
| Junior roast beef sandwich | 9.0 |
| Roast beef sandwich | 15.0 |
| Turkey sandwich | 24.0 |

**Burger King**

| | |
|---|---|
| Apple pie | 12.0 |
| Cheeseburger | 17.0 |
| Cheeseburger, double | 32.0 |
| French fries, regular | 11.0 |
| Hamburger | 13.0 |
| Onion rings, regular | 16.0 |
| Shake, chocolate | 10.0 |
| Shake, vanilla | 11.0 |
| Whopper | 36.0 |
| Whopper, with cheese | 45.0 |
| Whopper, double beef | 52.0 |
| Whopper, double beef, with cheese | 60.0 |
| Whopper Junior | 20.0 |
| Whopper Junior, with cheese | 25.0 |

**Dairy Queen**

| | |
|---|---|
| Banana split | 15.0 |
| Buster bar | 22.0 |
| Cheeseburger | 14.0 |
| Chili dog | 20.0 |
| Chocolate sundae, medium | 7.0 |
| Dilly bar | 15.0 |
| Fish sandwich | 17.0 |

| | |
|---|---|
| Float | 8.0 |
| Freeze | 13.0 |
| French fries, regular | 10.0 |
| Frozen dessert | 6.0 |
| Hamburger | 9.0 |
| Hamburger, super | 48.0 |
| Hot dog | 15.0 |
| Hot fudge brownie | 22.0 |
| Ice cream in cone | |
|     small | 3.0 |
|     medium | 7.0 |
|     large | 10.0 |
| Ice cream dipped in chocolate | |
|     small | 7.0 |
|     medium | 13.0 |
|     large | 20.0 |
| Ice cream sandwich | 4.0 |
| Onion rings | 17.0 |
| Shake, small | 11.0 |
| Shake, medium | 20.0 |
| Shake, large | 28.0 |

**Jack in the Box**

| | |
|---|---|
| Apple turnover | 24.0 |
| Breakfast Jack sandwich | 13.0 |
| Cheeseburger | 15.0 |
| French fries | 15.0 |
| French toast | 29.0 |
| Hamburger, Jumbo Jack | 29.0 |
| Hamburger, regular | 11.0 |
| Mobey Jack sandwich | 26.0 |
| Omelet, ham and cheese | 23.0 |
| Onion rings | 23.0 |
| Pancakes | 27.0 |

| | |
|---|---|
| Scrambled eggs | 44.0 |
| Shake, chocolate | 10.0 |
| Taco | 11.0 |

### Kentucky Fried Chicken

| | |
|---|---|
| Breast | 11.7 |
| Breast, extra crispy | 17.8 |
| Breast, fillet sandwich | 22.5 |
| Coleslaw | 7.5 |
| French fries | 6.7 |
| Gravy | 1.8 |
| Leg and thigh dinner | 35.2 |
| Leg and thigh dinner, extra crispy | 44.0 |
| Thigh | 17.5 |
| Wing | 9.0 |
| Wing and thigh dinner | 37.8 |
| Wing and thigh dinner, extra crispy | 48.2 |

### McDonald's

| | |
|---|---|
| Big Mac | 27.0 |
| Cheeseburger | 13.0 |
| Chicken McNuggets (6 pieces) | 20.0 |
| Cookies, Choc Chip (56 g) | 14.9 |
| Cookies, McDonaldland (56 g) | 9.8 |
| Egg McMuffin | 14.0 |
| Filet-o-Fish | 14.0 |
| French fries (8.3 g) | 11.5 |
| Hamburger | 8.8 |
| Hash browns | 7.0 |
| Hot cakes with butter and syrup | 10.0 |
| Quarter Pounder | 21.7 |
| Quarter Pounder, with cheese | 30.7 |
| Sausage, pork | 20.0 |
| Scrambled eggs | 10.0 |
| Fat-Wise™ muffin (100 g) | 5.7 |

### Taco Bell

| | |
|---|---|
| Burrito, bean | 10.8 |
| Burrito, beef | 21.0 |
| Burrito, combination | 16.0 |
| Burrito, supreme | 22.0 |
| Enchirito | 16.9 |
| Frijoles with cheese | 6.0 |
| Taco | 8.6 |
| Tostada | 6.0 |
| Tostada with beef | 15.0 |

### Wendy's

| | |
|---|---|
| Cheeseburger, single | 34.0 |
| Cheeseburger, double | 48.0 |
| Cheeseburger, triple | 68.0 |
| Chili con carne | 8.0 |
| French fries | 16.0 |
| Hamburger, single | 26.0 |
| Hamburger, double | 40.0 |
| Hamburger, triple | 51.0 |
| Shake, chocolate (frozen dessert) | 16.0 |

# Index